The
CASSEROLE
QUEENS
Cookbook

The CASSEROLE QUEENS Cookbook

put some lovin' in your oven
WITH 100 EASY ONE-DISH RECIPES

crystal cook
&
sandy pollock

CLARKSON POTTER/PUBLISHERS
NEW YORK

CLARKSON POTTER is a trademark and POTTER with colophon is a
registered trademark of Random House, Inc.

Casserole Queens is a registered trademark of Casserole Queens, LLC.

Library of Congress Cataloging-in-Publication Data
Cook, Crystal, and Sandy Pollock.
The casserole queens cookbook / [by Crystal Cook and Sandy Pollock].
Includes index.
1. Casserole cooking.   2. Cookbooks.   I. Cook, Crystal.   II. Title.
TX693.P63   2011
641.8'21—dc22   2010040541

ISBN 978-0-307-71785-6
eISBN 978-0-307-95339-1

Printed in the United States of America

Design by Amy Sly
Front cover photograph copyright © 2011 by Michael Lovitt

10 9 8 7 6 5 4 3 2 1

First Edition

This book was inspired by the stories, memories, and traditions of our childhoods. From the heartfelt to the humorous, they simply would not exist if it weren't for the loving homes we grew up in. We would like to dedicate this book to our parents—Joe Kent and Charlotte Cook, and Max and Margie Pollock—for always making mealtime more than just nourishment, but about family.

Contents

Introduction

Meet the Casserole Queens

Meet Crystal. Meet Sandy. Together we're bringing back the classic American casserole, along with other familiar recipes from a bygone era, and updating them with a retro-chic, gourmet flair. It's the best of the '50s with a modern, sophisticated twist. We call it *sophistakitsch*.

We know what you're thinking. It's not the 1950s, and the idea of whipping up a home-cooked meal with a freshly powdered face seems unreal. But wait! You *can* have that wholesome dinner ready for your family to devour! And guess what? You'll actually enjoy doing it. Don't think you have to throw on an apron and cook every night of the week (although we think it's fun!).

We have loads of nifty tips, creative shortcuts, and easy-to-cook meals that are designed to fit your hectic lifestyle. You may be on a budget, or have zero time to cook, but still yearn for a meal that's healthy and filling. Or maybe you're feeling adventurous and want to step it up a notch. (If so, you're in luck—we've included some of our best, world-class recipes derived from Sandy's training at the French Culinary Institute. The Queens are crafty like that.)

Whether it's a dinner party with friends, an evening meal with the family, or an all-out extravaganza, we hope our unique and quirky perspective, along with our delectable recipes, will inspire you to enjoy an evening gathered around the dinner table. And just maybe you'll find out what little Johnny is learning in science class.

Our Story

Let's back up a bit to a warm, summer night in Austin, Texas. Lots of folks have asked us how we got our business started, and the truth is that the idea for the Casserole Queens was conceived one night while contemplating life over a salty margarita (or two). (See "Idea-Generating Margaritas," opposite.)

As we sipped, Sandy spoke of how she was charmed by a recent holiday visit with her family. Sandy had decided to make all the Pollocks' signature dishes with her mom and siblings. The food was heavenly and the conversation centered on the good memories generated by these favorite recipes. She described the evening (while Crystal continued to sip), and proposed the idea of a business designed to help bring families back together around the dinner table with home-cooked goodness. Crystal, being from the South, couldn't agree more. Food and family go hand-in-hand where she grew up. In a world where people are always in a hurry and have little time for dinners together, the idea of convenient home-cooked meals is something that Sandy and Crystal both truly believed in. Hence, the Casserole Queens was born.

Now, we aren't saying that all great ideas start this way, but we have been delivering fresh-from-scratch meals to customers in Austin for over four years, all the while sporting heels, aprons, and the timeless tradition of mom's best recipes. Our business has been featured in numerous publications. Heck, we've even been on national television, appearing on the Food Network's *Throwdown! with Bobby Flay*.

Idea-Generating Margaritas

Careful! Drinking more than two of these can make your ideas seem better than they actually are.

MAKES 2 SERVINGS

Lime wedge

Sea salt

3 ounces premium silver tequila

3 ounces fresh lime juice

3 ounces fresh orange juice

1 ounce Triple Sec

1 Run the lime wedge around the rim of a margarita glass, and then roll the rim in the sea salt. Add fresh crushed ice to glass and set aside.

2 Fill a cocktail shaker with crushed ice. Add tequila, lime juice, orange juice, and Triple Sec. Shake vigorously, then pour over ice in a salt-rimmed glass. Let the ideas roll!

The Kitschy Kitchen
Retro Tips and How-To's

To us, casseroles represent more than just a delicious and nutritious meal for the family. They also represent a way of life—part of the retro-chic brand that defines the Casserole Queens as a business and the two of us as individuals. When we think of the quintessential 1950s homemaker, we have to chuckle. Hurry, ladies! Rush and fluff the pillows, prepare his favorite drink, straighten your hair, and quiet down the kids—your husband is coming home from a hard day at work! Oh, how times have changed. Homemakers may be men or women, and few of us would seek advice on creating a comfortable environment for our spouse. And yet the kitchen remains an important place in many of our lives, not because we are expected to be there but because it is where we can show our devotion to the ones we love most.

When you choose to express yourself through the dishes you cook, it's about more than the ingredients. It's about passion, presentation, creation, and pleasing the senses. (Mmmm, smell that? That's my cookin'!)

Having the right items on hand to prepare a quick, delicious meal is key. But also, taking steps to appropriately equip and use your kitchen makes the time you spend there more enjoyable and fulfilling. The kitchen has always been a creative, fun environment for us—cooking and dancing like no one is watching. This section was created with care to ensure you never get stuck in a cooking rut! Use our handy tips to minimize fuss, avoid cooking "emergencies," and create meals that fit your family's budget, tastes, preferences, and time constraints. We hope to ignite your inner artist, sparking a culinary creativity you never knew you had. Or at the very least, help you cook a solid, memorable meal.

Let's Dish

Casseroles may have become popular in the 1950s as a way to relieve women of kitchen drudgery, but they were also a response to a more active and social lifestyle. We, on the other hand, think they became popular because they were a way to "one-up" your friends and neighbors by appearing at the potluck dinner with the most colorful dish!

In our kitchen, we celebrate the casserole dish any which way we can. To be completely honest, we have a fairly loose interpretation of what the casserole dish actually is. If it all goes in one dish, then it is a casserole. From the old-school 9 x 13-inch glass Pyrex, to the highly decorated soufflé dish, Dutch oven, ramekin, or pie pan, it's all comfort—it's all a casserole.

In addition to brightening your own table, these dishes make wonderful host/hostess gifts. Ding! Now you know what to get that person who's impossible to shop for. There are so many super-cute and affordable vintage dishes available on the Internet, the next time you're invited to a potluck, bring your contribution in a dish that can be left with the host as a gift! And if swanky is the look you're going for, check out a new fad called the *casserole tote*. Made from amazing vintage fabrics, these totes make for easy transport and have real down-home appeal. They're chic and sassy, and easy to make.

Find One That Suits Your Style!

The beauty of the casserole dish is its variety. You can find them in every shape, size, color, or pattern. Go on, girl, get crazy—express yourself! You'll find that our recipes mostly call for a 9 x 13-inch dish, which is a nice, standard size. But with so many fun options, you can match your casserole to any mood or occasion.

GLASS. Keeping it real. We love this no-fuss, family favorite because glass dishes are inexpensive, and many come with plastic, airtight lids for easy transport and leftover storage. They are great for freezing and easy to clean up, and most are dishwasher safe.

PORCELAIN. The entertainer. Available in an array of colors and sizes, ovenproof, microwave proof, and dishwasher safe, these dishes can go from freezer to oven, then straight to the table. Soufflé dishes, shallow gratin dishes, and—our favorite—the ramekin all find places in our cupboards. Ah, ramekins—an oh-so-versatile dish that is a must in any kitchen. Perfect for individual-size meals and desserts, ramekins can also be used to serve condiments at the dinner table, like dipping sauces, toppings, or fresh sea salt or cracked black peppercorns. (Yes, we are in love.)

DUTCH OVEN. The old-fashioned gourmet sidekick. Aside from the ramekin, the Dutch oven is a heavy contender for our second favorite dish. This sturdy pot doesn't speak Dutch nor is it an oven, but it is a deep pot with a secure lid that can go from the stove top directly into the oven. Dutch ovens are well suited for long, slow cooking, such as for roasts, stews, and (yep, you guessed it!) casseroles. When we talk about Dutch ovens, we are referring to the modern enameled cast-iron version that does not need to be seasoned before use. These enameled Dutch ovens come in different shapes and sizes, and can usually be cleaned like ordinary cookware. Some brands may even be placed in the dishwasher. Get ready for a tricep toner, because once you fill this dish with food, it can be quite heavy.

Dress the Part

Imagine cooking the perfect dinner, with perfectly coiffed hair, red lipstick, a full skirt, and high heels. Okay, now snap out of it! We all know that June Cleaver left the kitchen years ago, but there is something to be said about feeling "put together" and in charge of your environment. For the Queens, a fun, flirty apron can transport you to another age, relaxed and comforted. We love aprons. Not only are they practical, but even on a rushed day, you can throw on an apron and feel a little more in control. As with everything we recommend, get one to match your personality. Maybe an apron with pockets is perfect for you, especially if you use it to store fun-size chocolates. Or perhaps you want to spice things up a bit in pink chiffon. It's all you!

Get into the Groove!

Music is a must when we cook. Our portable iPod speakers have a permanent home in our kitchen. The kitchen is our kingdom—and in our land, we sing and dance just as well as Beyoncé. Music sets the mood for energy and can also inspire and spur ideas. It just makes cooking that much more fun! Apart from the cuisine, there are few components more important than the right music. Music helps your guests relax and puts you in the proper entertaining mood. Choose tunes that match the ethnicity or region of your dish.

Need a microphone quick? Grab a big serving spoon or spatula.

Dish-Towel Apron

Sandy's family does a lot of group cooking during the holidays. One year, Sandy's sister Yvette made aprons for all the girls in the Pollock family. The aprons were made from an assortment of Christmas-themed dish towels, with red and green ribbons for tying. We all loved them so much and still wear them to this day. Make them for someone you love!

MATERIALS NEEDED

1 dish towel

2 yard-long pieces of ribbon (to accommodate any size body)

2 big buttons

Scissors

A needle

Thread

STEP 1 **ATTACH BUTTONS**

On the best side of the dish towel, sew a button to each top corner of one long side.

STEP 2 **TIE RIBBON**

Tie a piece of ribbon around each button, leaving a little tail. This will make it easy to remove the ribbons before washing the apron, which will keep them from unraveling.

STEP 3 **WEAR IT**

To wear the apron, wrap the ribbons around your waist as many times as necessary and tie a bow.

STEP 4 **ENJOY!**

Be Prepared

A well-stocked kitchen can be a lifesaver when you need to whip up dinner at a moment's notice. Here are some things we suggest keeping on hand, especially when there's an impatient crew on deck.

THINGS IN CANS. Don't laugh, we are serious! Items such as tuna, sliced black olives, green chiles, tomatoes, canned beans, and tomato sauces can be integral to any casserole meal. Regardless of what you might have heard, don't forget the cream soups. For some, cream soups conjure up bad casserole memories. We disagree. In fact, we appreciate their value and, when used with the right spices and fresh ingredients, you can make something quite good. We take pride in the need to keep things fresh and real, and there are times when we will encourage you to step it up a notch by inviting you to make your own soups and stocks from our "From Scratch" section of this book. But when life comes at you fast, these canned soups can be your best friend. They are the type of friends who would drive 1,000 miles to bail you out of a Mexican prison. And the fact is, just as we have grown up over the years, so have they. Most brands nowadays are heart healthy, offering low-fat and less-sodium versions.

SPICES. We encourage you to have myriad spices on hand. Not only are they handy when creating meals from leftovers but they are the magic that turns the staple family recipe into something you can call your own when you add a special twist. After all, cooking with herbs is like icing on a cake: it makes the dish complete. Herbs add that extra something that elevates everyday food.

ONIONS AND GARLIC. Onions and garlic play a role in almost all of our recipes. Cry if you have to, but we suggest having them on hand at all times. We always have shallots in our pantry, as well. Shallots, in our opinion, are the perfect blend of garlic and onion. Voilà!

YOUR FAVORITE CONDIMENTS. Stock your refrigerator and pantry with an assortment of condiments that you enjoy: mayonnaise, salsa, Tabasco, Worcestershire sauce, ketchup, and a variety of mustards. They always come in handy for rounding out or adding flavor to a recipe. Do a routine check every three months or so to make sure they are fresh.

BULK PROTEINS. Buy proteins such as red meat and poultry in bulk to keep them affordable. Meat freezes really well and can easily be stored in individual portions. Just remember to allow enough time to thaw these items in your refrigerator for maximum safety.

FROZEN VEGETABLES. We personally prefer to use fresh vegetables, but just as with canned soups, frozen vegetables work fine, too. While some consider frozen vegetables inferior to their fresh counterparts, the opposite is actually true in many cases. Vegetables purchased in the produce section of supermarkets have spent multiple days in transit, and many of the nutrients may have leeched out. Frozen vegetables are frozen at their freshest, thereby capturing these nutrients. They are also a good solution when money or time is tight, and they are available when the fresh stuff is out of season.

GRAINS AND STARCHES. For casserole toppings and hearty fillings, keep a variety of grains and starches in stock, such as pastas, rice, crackers, bread crumbs, cereals, and potatoes.

OILS, VINEGARS, AND COOKING SPRAYS. A variety of oils is key for sautéing and adding flavor. Vinegar is perfect when a little acidity is needed. Nonstick sprays are handy for greasing dishes and cutting calories.

EGGS AND DAIRY. Most casseroles are held together by eggs and dairy, so you'll need to have fresh eggs, milk, butter, sour cream, and a selection of your favorite cheeses.

BAKING SUPPLIES. All-purpose flour, light and dark brown sugars, granulated sugar, baking powder, baking soda, and cornstarch should always be in your kitchen. Aside from baking batches of yummy treats, you'll find these ingredients in a number of casserole recipes to make and thicken sauces.

WINE. *"A bottle of red, a bottle of white. It all depends upon your appetite."* As Mr. Billy Joel suggests, keep a bottle of red and a bottle of dry white wine on hand, for both your cooking and your drinking pleasure. If you don't use a lot of wine, the small four-pack of airplane-size wine bottles works extremely well.

Go-Go Kitchen Gadget

Now, we would like to take a moment to offer some insight into other items that make life in the kitchen a bit easier—our beloved tools of the trade. We could go on and on about all the different tools that you should have in your kitchen, but we won't send you out on that special paella pan mission just yet. Here are our top "must-have" suggestions for making things simpler in the kitchen.

THE RIGHT KNIVES. A collection of appropriate and sharp knives is a must, but hold off on spending your entire paycheck on a packaged block set. We swear on Mamaw's fried apple pie that you don't need it. You can get just about any job in the kitchen done with only a few key knives. We recommend the *all-purpose chef knife*, the *paring knife,* and the *serrated knife* (aka bread knife). Along with your knives, keep a pair of *kitchen shears*. From snipping twine and cutting flower stems to trimming vegetables and meats, a sharp pair of shears is indispensable.

LATEX GLOVES. Smack! Gloves are handier than you will ever know. For example, since Crystal's knife skills are lackluster at best, it has become her duty in the kitchen to bone the chickens while Sandy perfectly chops, dices, and minces for prep. The boning chore has sparked a deep love in Crystal for her latex gloves. Plus, it makes cross-contamination a nonissue. Make sure you don't have a latex allergy!

SHARPIES. Sandy says that every good chef always has a Sharpie on hand. Not only are these markers good for keeping your refrigerator/freezer inventory clearly labeled and up to date, but they are also fun for drawing mustaches on your business partner while she is boning chickens and is defenseless.

FOOD WRAPPERS. No kitchen (especially a casserole kitchen) is complete unless you have lots of aluminum foil, freezer bags, plastic wrap, and oodles of parchment and wax papers.

DISH TOWELS. You can never have too many for cleaning up messes and drying dishes or hands. We also like making aprons out of our favorite patterns (see page 17). They make nice everyday aprons that you don't worry about getting a little messy or wiping your hands on.

STORAGE CONTAINERS. We just love the sizes and affordable shapes available. We recommend having at least three large (2-quart) plastic, three medium (1-quart), and six smaller (2-cup or less) containers. A couple of glass ones are nice for onions and stinky cheeses, since plastic tends to hold on to odors. Another great tip: Tired of spaghetti sauce–stained plastic containers? Spray them with nonstick cooking spray first to prevent this food-stain faux pas.

CHEESE GRATER. Block cheeses are less expensive than the preshredded kinds. Grating your own cheese makes casserole cooking even more affordable.

ICE TRAYS. Ah, the forgotten ice tray! What a clever retro tool. Call up this old friend and use it for any leftover white wine (as if), chicken broth, or tomato sauce. Just fill ice cube trays and freeze them, then transfer the cubes to labeled freezer bags when done. Each cube is two tablespoons, so 2 cubes equal ¼ cup. Just place them in the pan while cooking to defrost them as needed.

WINE OPENER/BOTTLE OPENER. Do we need to say more?

How to Scale Appropriately

It's just as simple to make two casseroles as it is one (one for now, one for later), and they are easy to divide into individual, oven-safe containers. There are no hard-and-fast rules for scaling casseroles, but here are a few general guidelines. If you want to make:

INDIVIDUAL CASSEROLES: Prepare the ingredients according to the recipe, then distribute evenly into smaller oven-safe containers (ramekins work great and look adorable). Reduce cooking time by about 25 percent and watch closely.

LARGER CASSEROLES: Double a standard 9 x 13-inch casserole recipe and use a disposable 20 x 12-inch foil steam pan

Other Noteworthy Reasons to Scale and Freeze

- Your husband likes tofu, and your kids dig meat.

- Tired of dishpan hands? Cleanup is a cinch. Making casseroles beforehand means no mess in the kitchen that night. (You made that mess weeks ago, hooray!)

- You can't be a "hostess with the mostess" when you're all stressed out. Give the cook of the house more time to do the things she wants, like enjoy a glass of wine and a good conversation with family, friends, or guests.

- It's friendly on the family budget. Little Billy needs new gym shorts. Susie is in dire need of a sticker book. Casseroles are affordable—because we wouldn't dare take stickers away from a child.

(commonly used by restaurants and cafeterias). In this case, the thickness of the casserole doesn't change much, so the cooking time should be about the same. Allow extra time for large casseroles to thaw completely before cooking. (Note that you might want to measure your oven first; many won't accommodate a pan of this size.)

ADDITIONAL CASSEROLES USING THE ORIGINAL RECIPE SIZE (one for now, one for the freezer): Simply multiply the recipe by the total number of casseroles you're making. (Okay, so this one isn't rocket science.)

Note that these are only guidelines. All recipes and ovens are different. There is no substitute for keeping an eye on your casserole and watching for the telltale signs of doneness: the casserole should be bubbling around the edges, hot in the center, and brown on the top.

Hi-dee-ho, It's Off to the Freezer They Go!

We deliver dishes to our customers frozen, so we know the recipes that freeze well and the ones that don't. Throughout the book, we highlight the freezer-friendly casseroles that you can plan on making ahead of time.

Bye-bye, freezer burn. Here are some general tips for preparing, storing, and thawing frozen goods so that they will come out perfectly every time.

TO PREPARE

- We have found that the best way to freeze a casserole is at the stage right before baking, when all the ingredients have already been prepped and cooked and beautifully assembled in your favorite baking dish.

- We *do not* recommend freezing any seafood casseroles. It is best to enjoy seafood dishes fresh. Trust us on this one.

- Some casseroles call for crunchy toppings of crackers, cereals, french-fried onions, chips, and the like. Wait to add such toppings until right before baking, instead of putting them on before freezing. They tend to get soggy when frozen, and you miss out on the delightful crunch.

- Do not freeze previously baked pastry dough. Add fresh or frozen unbaked pastry during reheating. (Or freeze with unbaked dough in place.) Pastries are at their peak tastiness immediately after baking, and they just don't reheat well. Take this into consideration for leftovers, as well. If you aren't serving a crowd, make smaller portions in order to enjoy pastry at its best—fresh from the oven!

- If your casserole recipe calls for starchy ingredients such as pasta, rice, or beans, prepare them al dente, or slightly undercooked. Between freezing and the additional cook time in the oven, they can become "mushy" if not prepared correctly.

- Freeze casseroles either in quantities just right for your family or in individual servings. (See the portion control section on page 22 for more ideas on how to do this.)

TO FREEZE

- Low on casserole dishes? Keep what you have available by lining pans with heavy aluminum foil before assembling your recipe. Once it is frozen, you can simply lift it out of the dish and tuck it back into the freezer. Your dish is now ready for other upcoming projects. Not only does your casserole stay neatly wrapped in foil, in the freezer, but it also creates a lot more space for storing.

- Always keep in mind that you should cool your casseroles completely before freezing. A quick way to do this is by setting the casserole in a pan of ice water to cool it to room temperature. Take the time for this extra step, because if you put a casserole in the freezer hot, the outside of the dish will freeze quickly while the inside may not cool in time to prevent spoilage. Plus, you don't want to raise the temperature of your freezer and harm your other frozen goodies. Nobody likes melted ice cream!

- Cover your casseroles with freezer-friendly products such as freezer paper, heavy foil, or a tight-fitting lid. We don't use plastic wrap, as it sometimes sticks.

- Always have a permanent marker on hand to label the casserole with the contents, number of servings, and date of freezing.

TO SERVE

- To ensure quality, do not store your casserole in the freezer for longer than two months. You made it with love and fresh ingredients, so you'll want it to taste that way.

- Don't be tempted to cook your casseroles in the microwave—the dreaded flavor zapper. For best results—and to ensure that it cooks through—always bake in an oven.

- Frozen casseroles cook best when they're completely thawed. The best way to thaw a casserole before reheating is by letting it stand overnight in the refrigerator. Then cook as directed by the recipe. If the casserole is for some reason not completely thawed, bake an additional 15 to 30 minutes or until the center is hot.

- We realize that people sometimes stop by unannounced (gasp! there you stand in your sweats and mustard-stained T-shirt) and you may not have the luxury of thawing your casserole. You most certainly can cook a casserole without thawing it first, but keep in mind that it will take approximately double the time to cook.

- Do not refreeze casseroles after they have been cooked. Refrigerate any leftovers.

More Freezer Tips

Wait, there's more! Here are some useful freezer tips for staple casserole ingredients:

- We've found that soft cheeses are easier to cut when slightly frozen. Simply place the cheese in the freezer 20 to 30 minutes prior to shredding or cutting. The cheese will be easier to handle.

- Casserole recipes often call for creamed soups and fresh stocks. If you choose to make your own soups from scratch (see pages 200–203), chances are you will have extra on hand. For the most part, soups and broths freeze very well. Thaw the cream soups in a double boiler to prevent the cream from burning. Clear soups and broths can simply be thawed in a saucepan set over medium heat until heated thoroughly.

- Bread crumbs and croutons are always handy for adding texture to casseroles, but they can go stale quickly once opened. Keep them fresh longer by storing them in the freezer.

- Hey sugar, what's your story? Brown sugar is used often in our casseroles and can be kept fresh by storing in the freezer. Place in a freezer bag or other airtight container for maximum freshness. Don't worry if it hardens; it will soften up as it thaws.

- Make several batches of pie crusts at one time to save yourself some time later on. You can form dough into disks. Wrap them tightly in plastic wrap and freeze. When ready to use, remove from the freezer and allow to thaw before using. Another big time-saver is to roll the dough out between several sheets of plastic wrap. Using a small pizza box for the storage container, stack the disks, and then store the box in the freezer. Use as needed for your favorite recipe.

- Keep your nuts fresh longer by storing them in the freezer. Package both shelled and unshelled nuts in freezer bags and freeze up to six months. Other benefits for freezing nuts are that unshelled nuts will crack easier when frozen, and there is never a need to "thaw" nuts—they can go directly from the freezer into your dish.

- When cutting dried fruit, you will find that it sometimes sticks to the blade of your knife. Dried fruits stay fresh and moist when frozen and are easier to chop frozen. Another way to tackle this problem is to coat your knife with cooking spray.

Lighten Up: Quick Tips to Cut Calories

We understand that sometimes substitutions are necessary in life, and although we have recipes that cater specifically to a lighter lifestyle, here are some quick ways to kiss those calories good-bye. Nifty, I lost fifty!

Of course, when you alter a recipe, there may be some trial and error. Please keep in mind that, when making substitutions, the consistency or flavor of the dish can change slightly. So it might take a few times of testing on little Billy before you hit it out of the park.

- If a recipe calls for a canned fruit in heavy syrup, forget the can and substitute the real thing. If the fruit happens not to be in season, opt for a canned version in its natural juices.

- Okay, we admit it—we really love salt. But if you need to reduce or omit the salt in your diet, start experimenting with fresh herbs and spices. We also suggest looking for alternatives in our recipes by substituting soups and sauces. Most condensed soups like chicken broths, tomato sauces, and soy sauces are now available in low-sodium varieties. Or, if you have the time, you can always make your own.

- So maybe your mom was right when she told you to eat more veggies. Simply decrease the meat and increase the vegetables called for in the recipe. Or, if you are feeling adventurous, there are a lot of healthful soy-based meat alternatives. Seriously, we've tried them and they do a fine job standing in for the real deal! We are big fans of Morning Star and Bocca brands.

- Use egg whites or egg substitutes in place of whole eggs. (Two egg whites equal one egg, and ¼ cup of egg substitute equals one egg.)

- Foods that are white in color are usually hiding a dirty secret: empty carbs. Choose whole-grain versions of pasta and bread. Wheat flour over white flour. Substitute white rice with brown rice, wild rice, bulgar, or pearl barley.

- Many casseroles are topped with a layer of cheese. Experiment with reduced-fat cheeses by combining low-fat grated cheeses with whole-wheat bread crumbs. We recommend this method over using the fat-free kind. Fat-free cheese products tend not to melt and taste rubbery. Buy part-skim mozzarella and/or feta cheeses, which are naturally lower in fat. Or, if all else fails, you can simply use less cheese than the recipe calls for. Brilliant!

- In the grocery store, look for lean meats and skinless poultry. Reduced-fat or turkey sausage and bacon are also good options.

- When baking your favorite sweets, substitute applesauce or prune puree for half the butter, shortening, or oil called for in the recipe. It works really well. But as we mentioned, it might take a few tries to get it just right!

- If you haven't noticed, the Casserole Queens love cooking spray. When we cook at home, we always grease our pans with cooking spray rather than butter, oil, or shortening. Another good tip: when recipes call for sautéing vegetables with oil, substitute cooking spray to reduce the fat.

- Try substituting low-fat 1 or 2 percent milk when a recipe calls for milk. Skim milk will work, too, but it may not thicken as well when cooked. In cases where a recipe calls for cream, try replacing all or part of it with evaporated skim milk.

- Use a low-fat or nonfat mayonnaise, sour cream, cream cheese, yogurt, and cottage cheese in recipes calling for them.

How to Use this Cookbook

Basic Recipe Assumptions and Techniques

Wondering what we mean by this? Well, maybe this little story about Crystal's grandmother—or, as we say in the South, "Mamaw"—can help clarify. Mamaw Cook was an amazing cook (with an appropriate last name), and her claim to fame was delicious, melt-in-your-mouth fried apple pies. Everyone adored them, so it was only natural that the family asked Mamaw for the recipe. The funny thing was—there wasn't one. "A pinch of this," a "handful of that," and still to this day, no one can come close to making them taste as special as she did.

So how does this story relate to the Queens? Well, we kind of work the same way. Like most great chefs, Sandy likes to cook intuitively, and with the help of her trusty sidekick Crystal, she experiments until the dish is mastered. We have taken great care to ensure the list of ingredients and preparations for each recipe are correct. Chances are, you won't be in the kitchen with us, so even though we take the time to detail instructions in our recipes, below you will find some generalities and techniques that are always good to keep in mind—even when not making our recipes.

BLANCHING: To impart the most flavor into your vegetables, we recommend blanching them in salty water. Here's how to do it: Fill a large pot with water, heavily salt it (should taste like the sea), and bring to a boil over high heat. Add the vegetables and boil until they start to soften, usually about 3 minutes. Lightly poke at the vegetables with a knife; when you can break the skin without much resistance, you know they're done. Now pour them into a strainer, and plunge the strainer into a large bowl of ice water. The cold water will stop the cooking immediately and help the veggies retain texture and color. Drain the vegetables and pat dry.

PROTEINS: Proteins such as ground beef, chicken, and pork are always seasoned with salt and pepper.

SEAFOOD: When working with seafood, you'll notice that it tends to get a little watery when cooked. Prior to cooking, please rinse, thoroughly drain, and pat seafood dry with paper towels before preparing. This will help tremendously.

PASTA AND RICE: Boil these items in salted water to season them, unless it is a recipe in the light section.

BUTTER: We always use unsalted butter so that we are controlling the amount of salt in the recipe. We like to be in control.

OVEN TEMPS: Your oven varies from Mrs. Henderson's oven down the road, so think of our baking times as basic guidelines. Cooking times may vary ever so slightly, so please pay attention during cooking. Check the casseroles a few times near the end of baking to look for bubbling at the edges and a hot center.

DANCING: We find that dancing while cooking helps a great deal. We are personally big fans of the Robot, but we have found that the Cabbage Patch tends to work just as well. Trust us.

Friendly Faces

I spy a helpful icon. Just to make your life even easier, we've created some memorable, helpful icons scattered throughout this book. With a glance, you will quickly know more important information about the recipe you're planning to whip up. Here's the legend that tells you what the icons mean, so you know exactly what to look for!

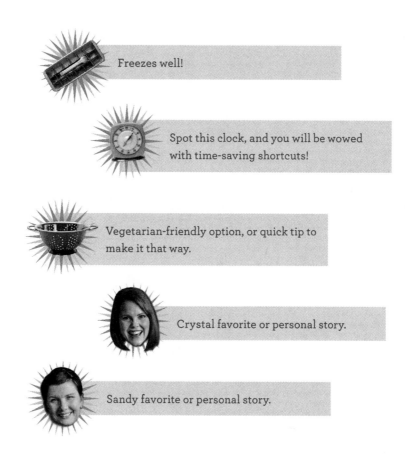

Freezes well!

Spot this clock, and you will be wowed with time-saving shortcuts!

Vegetarian-friendly option, or quick tip to make it that way.

Crystal favorite or personal story.

Sandy favorite or personal story.

Fun for the Whole Family. Neat-O!

Remember the days when there was nothing better to do but prepare delicious, home-cooked meals for your family? Yeah, neither do we. Those days may be gone, but with our easy, classic recipes, cooking doesn't have to be a full-time job.

Bringing families together around the dinner table is what we do, and with these dishes, yours will come running. Who doesn't love a good, home-cooked meal? Remember Grandma's chicken pot pie? Your mom's tuna noodle surprise? Some of these recipes may be familiar to you. They may even take you back. The flavors, however, are current—bold, fresh, and updated to modern tastes. And with a few of our time-saving tweaks, you can enjoy these classic dishes without spending all afternoon in the kitchen. June Cleaver was fictional, anyway.

Meatball Casserole

CQ's Royal Cottage Pie

Beef Stroganoff

Traditional King Ranch Casserole

Pork Chops with Sauerkraut

Corn Dog Casserole

Deep-Dish Pizza, Chicago Style

World's Greatest Chicken Pot Pie

Valley-Style Arroz con Pollo

"Keep Austin Weird"
Spam Casserole

Tuna Noodle Casserole

Shrimply Delicious Shrimp
and Grits

Baked Four-Cheese Pasta

Mamaw's Stuffed Peppers

Easy Eggplant Parmesan

Jayne's Baked Spaghetti

Meatball Casserole

MAKES 6 SERVINGS

Cooking spray

1 pound ground beef

1 cup saltine cracker crumbs

¼ cup chopped onion

¼ cup chopped green bell pepper

½ teaspoon salt

¼ teaspoon freshly ground black pepper

1 large egg, lightly beaten

1 (10¾-ounce) can mushroom soup, or 1½ cups homemade Cream of Mushroom Soup (page 203)

1 cup whole milk

1 tablespoon vegetable oil

⅓ cup all-purpose flour

½ cup chili sauce (such as Heinz)

It usually hits you from out of nowhere. You walk into a kitchen and bam!—there it is—a smell so welcoming and so familiar that you find yourself transported to another time and place. Smells are magical like that. Every time Sandy starts to make this dish, her mind becomes filled with fond memories from her childhood of meals shared with her trio of sisters, Yvonne, Yvette, and Kellye. This was her family's favorite meal growing up, and we hope that it will create as many sweet memories for you as it has for Sandy.

Don't confuse chili sauce with hot pepper sauce or canned chili (been there, done that!). Chili sauce is found in the grocery next to ketchup.

We suggest serving this casserole over rice. Try our recipe on page 195.

1 Preheat the oven to 350°F. Lightly coat a 9 x 13-inch casserole dish with cooking spray.

2 Combine the ground beef, cracker crumbs, onion, bell peppers, salt, pepper, and egg in a large mixing bowl. In a separate bowl, combine the soup and milk. Add half of the soup mixture to the meat mixture and mix well.

3 Heat the oil in a large sauté pan set over medium-high heat. Form the meat mixture into balls. Toss each meatball in the flour and shake off any excess. Working in batches, cook the meatballs in the hot oil, turning to brown all sides, about 10 minutes. Don't overcrowd the pan. Transfer the meatballs to the prepared casserole dish.

4 Combine the chili sauce and the remaining soup mixture; pour over the meatballs. Bake for 30 minutes or until the liquid is bubbling and light brown on top.

The meatballs for this casserole freeze well. Prepare them ahead of time by rolling them out and putting them in the bottom of a casserole dish. Use wax paper to separate layers, if needed. When you're ready to make the casserole, thaw the meatballs and follow the recipe starting with heating the oil.

It's a Pollock family tradition to eat lunch together on Sunday afternoons, and Sandy's mom always puts together an amazing spread for everyone. Front and center at many of these Sunday meals is this meatball casserole. Enjoy!

CQ's Royal Cottage Pie

MAKES 8 TO 10 SERVINGS

2 pounds russet potatoes (about 4 medium), peeled and cut into 1-inch pieces

½ cup (1 stick) unsalted butter, softened

1 cup heavy cream, warmed

4 ounces sharp Cheddar cheese, grated (1 cup)

Salt and freshly ground black pepper

2 pounds ground beef

1 medium onion, finely chopped

1 medium carrot, peeled and diced

½ teaspoon salt

2 medium garlic cloves, minced

¼ cup all-purpose flour

1 tablespoon tomato paste

2 cups beef broth (see page 201)

4 teaspoons Worcestershire sauce

1½ teaspoons finely chopped fresh thyme

1 (15-ounce) can whole kernel corn, drained

1 cup frozen peas

Ah, the never-ending debate of shepherd's pie versus cottage pie. So, what's the difference? It's all about the meat. A shepherd's pie traditionally calls for lamb, and a cottage pie calls for beef (or sometimes only vegetables). We wouldn't think of calling our meat pie a shepherd's pie, as we'd rather keep ourselves out of the line of fire. The beauty of this meal is that it's a great way to use leftovers. Include what you have on hand, whether beef or lamb, or even just a great mix of vegetables. Our favorite interpretation is below, so once you master the steps, try your hand at a variation.

✳ ✳ ✳ ✳ ✳

1 Preheat the oven to 400°F.

2 For the topping, put the potatoes in a large saucepan, cover with water, and bring to a boil over high heat. Reduce the heat to low and simmer until the potatoes are tender and a fork inserted into the center meets little resistance, 15 to 20 minutes.

3 Drain the potatoes and return them to the saucepan set over low heat. Mash the potatoes thoroughly with a potato masher. Fold in the butter until melted, then stir in the warm cream and cheese. Season with salt and pepper to taste. Cover the pan and set aside.

4 For the filling, season the beef with salt and pepper. Cook the beef in a 10-inch ovenproof skillet set over medium heat, breaking up any lumps with the back of a spoon, until it is browned thoroughly, about 10 minutes. Drain the beef, discarding all but 1 tablespoon of the rendered fat, and set aside.

5 Heat the 1 tablespoon of reserved beef fat in the same skillet set over medium heat until shimmering. Add the onion, carrot, and salt, and cook until the vegetables are soft, 5 to 7 minutes. Stir in the garlic and cook until fragrant, about 30 seconds. Stir in the flour and tomato paste and cook, stirring constantly, until the flour is cooked, about 1 minute. Slowly stir in the broth, Worcestershire sauce, and thyme, scraping up the browned bits on the bottom of the pan. Bring the mixture to a simmer, reduce the heat to medium low, and cook until the sauce has thickened, 3 to 5 minutes.

6 Remove the pan from the heat, stir in the reserved cooked beef, the corn, and peas, and season to taste with salt and pepper. Pour the filling into a 9 x 13-inch casserole dish, smoothing it into an even layer. Dollop the potato topping evenly over the filling, then spread it into an even layer. Bake for 30 minutes or until warmed through.

Adding warmed cream, versus cold, to the potatoes will keep them from becoming gummy. Sandy learned this great tip while working at Jeffrey's, a restaurant in Austin, and ever since, she's had a much improved relationship with mashed potatoes.

Beef Stroganoff

MAKES 8 TO 10 SERVINGS

Cooking spray

1 (12-ounce) bag wide egg noodles

2 tablespoons unsalted butter

Salt and freshly ground black pepper

1 pound boneless round steak, cut into ¾-inch cubes

½ cup all-purpose flour

1 (10-ounce) container sliced button mushrooms

½ cup chopped onion

3 garlic cloves, minced

1 (10¾-ounce) can condensed tomato soup

1 cup sour cream

2 cups grated Parmesan cheese (8 ounces)

1 tablespoon Worcestershire sauce

10 drops Tabasco sauce

½ teaspoon salt

½ teaspoon freshly ground black pepper

From Russia with love! Our stroganoff has all the velvety richness of the original comfort-food favorite, with just a little kick (we can't help ourselves—we're from Texas, where Tabasco sauce is practically a food group). Our secret ingredient is tomato soup! We added the soup to brighten up the overall flavor of the dish. But don't worry, our variation of this classic is still enough to make you want to Cossack-dance your way back for seconds.

1 Preheat the oven to 350°F. Lightly coat a 9 x 13-inch casserole dish with cooking spray and set aside.

2 Cook the pasta according to package directions. Drain and set aside. Keep warm.

3 Melt 1 tablespoon of the butter in a large skillet set over medium-high heat. Season the beef with salt and pepper, then dredge in the flour, shaking off the excees. Place the steak cubes in the skillet and cook, turning, until browned on all sides, about 10 minutes. Transfer the meat to the prepared casserole dish. In the same skillet, add the mushrooms, onion, garlic, and remaining 1 tablespoon of butter. Cook, stirring, until the onion and garlic soften and the mushrooms start to get a little color, about 8 minutes.

4 In a medium bowl, combine the tomato soup, sour cream, ½ cup of the Parmesan cheese, the Worcestershire sauce, Tabasco sauce, salt, and pepper. Add the onion mixture, stir to combine, and pour over the meat in the casserole dish.

5 Bake for 45 minutes or until the meat is tender. Sprinkle with remaining cheese and bake an additional 15 minutes. Serve hot over egg noodles.

Traditional King Ranch Casserole

The King Ranch Casserole is as much a part of Texas history as the Alamo. So imagine when Crystal—originally from Georgia—marched into Sandy's kitchen with some ideas on how to improve the dish. Yep, you guessed it. Disaster. You just can't mess with Texas. Our recipe hasn't budged from the original, which has been in Sandy's family for as long as she can remember. Our fellow Austinites share the same love for this traditional recipe and have made the King Ranch one of our most popular menu items. Enjoy!

1 Preheat the oven to 350°F.

2 In a large saucepan set over medium-high heat, combine the cream of chicken soup, cream of mushroom soup, chicken broth, tomatoes, and garlic salt. Stir until warm, about 5 minutes. Remove from the heat and set aside.

3 Grease a 9 x 13-inch baking dish with cooking spray. Put half of the tortillas in the bottom of the pan. Layer in half each of the chicken meat and onion, then sprinkle with one-third of the cheese mix. Pour half of the soup mixture over the top, then repeat the layers. Top the casserole with the remaining third of the cheese.

4 Bake for 45 minutes or until the cheese has melted and browned slightly.

MAKES 8 SERVINGS

1 (10¾-ounce) can cream of chicken soup, or 1½ cups homemade Cream of Chicken Soup (page 202)

1 (10¾-ounce) can cream of mushroom soup, or 1½ cups homemade Cream of Mushroom Soup (page 203)

1 cup chicken broth (see page 200)

1 (10-ounce) can Rotel tomatoes or diced tomatoes with green chiles

1 teaspoon garlic salt

Cooking spray

12 (8-inch) corn tortillas, cut into quarters

1 (3-pound) roasted chicken, boned and shredded (see page 204)

1 medium onion, diced

2 cups store-bought grated Mexican-blend cheese (8 ounces)

Great for freezing! See our Freezer Tips on pages 23–27.

Pork Chops with Sauerkraut

MAKES 6 SERVINGS

Cooking spray

10 slices bacon

2 (14-ounce) cans sauerkraut or homemade (recipe follows)

6 ½-inch-thick pork chops

Salt and freshly ground black pepper

4 russet potatoes, cut into ¼-inch-thick slices

2 medium onions, sliced

1 (14¾-ounce) can stewed tomatoes

Crystal's mother's maiden name is German. Well, actually it was Germaine, but the name was changed when her ancestors settled in South Carolina. The locals refused to call them "Germaine," and instead just said "that German family." To celebrate the German/Germaine family, we like to grab our favorite lager and whip out this traditional dish. The recipe calls for prepared sauerkraut, but if you like the idea of making your own, check out Crystal's family recipe (see opposite).

※　※　※　※　※

1 Preheat the oven to 350°F. Coat a 9 x 13-inch casserole dish with cooking spray.

2 Line the bottom of the casserole dish with bacon. Scatter the sauerkraut over the bacon. Season the pork chops with salt and pepper, then lay them on top. Layer the potato and onion slices over the pork, then scatter the tomatoes over the top. Bake the casserole for 2 hours or until the potatoes are tender.

That German Family Sauerkraut

Some simply don't have the patience to wait the weeks necessary for sauerkraut to ferment, but we prefer this old-school way of preparing it. The wait was actually a big part of the fun when Crystal was a kid (apparently there wasn't much to do in the North Georgia mountains).

Pack the cabbage into sterilized quart jars. Add 1 teaspoon of pickling salt to each jar and cover with water. Place the lid and bands on the jars and close as tightly as you can by hand. You might want to place your jars on a baking sheet or in a shallow dish, because during the fermenting process the lids will loosen and juice will run down the sides of the jars. This is why you don't seal them completely airtight as you do when you are canning. Store in a dry dark place to ferment for 3 weeks. Crystal's family stored theirs in their basement, which added to the fun (it was so scary down there!). If you do not have a basement, use a pantry or cover them with a towel.

MAKES 4 TO 6 QUARTS

1 head of green cabbage, chopped

4 to 6 quart canning jars with lids

4 to 6 teaspoons pickling salt (non-iodized)

Corn Dog

Casserole

MAKES 6 TO 8 SERVINGS

Cooking spray

2 tablespoons unsalted butter

2 cups finely chopped celery

1½ cups sliced green onions,
green parts only

1 pound hot dogs

1½ cups whole milk

2 large eggs

2 (8½-ounce) boxes Jiffy corn
muffin mix

2 teaspoons chopped fresh sage

¼ teaspoon salt

¼ teaspoon freshly ground
black pepper

8 ounces sharp Cheddar
cheese, shredded (2 cups)

Ah, the Corn Dog Casserole! Just the smell alone will get the kids
to the table in time for dinner. Maybe even your neighbor's kids.
Okay, forget the kids. Who are we kidding? If you've ever dropped
by your local carnival or street fair just to get yourself a corn dog,
this is the dish for you! It's fun to act like a kid sometimes, anyway.

1 Preheat the oven to 400°F. Lightly coat a 9 x 13-inch
casserole dish with cooking spray.

2 Melt the butter in a large sauté pan set over medium heat.
Add the celery and cook for 5 minutes. Add the green
onions and cook for 2 more minutes. Transfer the celery
and green onions to a large bowl and set aside.

3 Cut the hot dogs in half lengthwise, then cut into ½-inch
pieces. Sauté the hot dogs in same pan, set over medium-
high heat, turning to brown on all sides, about 7 minutes.
Transfer to the bowl with celery and green onions. Set aside.

4 Lightly beat the milk and eggs together. Add the corn
muffin mix, sage, salt, and pepper. Add 1½ cups of the
cheese and combine.

5 Put the hot dog mixture in the bottom of the prepared
casserole dish. Pour in the corn muffin mix mixture and
sprinkle the remaining ½ cup of cheese over the top. Bake
for 30 minutes or until the top is golden brown, set, and
risen slightly.

Great for freezing! See our Freezer Tips on pages 23–27.

 This can easily be converted into a vegetarian dish by substituting your favorite vegetarian hot dogs.

 Corn dogs instantly take Sandy back to summers in the Valley. As soon as the last school bell rang, she and her sisters would run out to meet her parents for their annual trip to the local wholesale food distributor. (The distributor supplied food in bulk to restaurants, and generally did not sell to regular people—but that didn't stop Marge, Sandy's mom.) Her parents stocked up on burritos, pickles, and hamburger patties to feed the family over the summer, while the girls begged nonstop for the mammoth box of frozen corn dogs. Eventually, Marge and Max would cave in, and the girls would giggle in delight. The summer was then full of afternoons eating tasty corn dogs covered in lots of yellow mustard. Yum!

Deep-Dish Pizza, Chicago Style

MAKES 6 TO 8 SERVINGS

Cooking spray

3 teaspoons olive oil

1 pound hot Italian pork sausage, casings removed

1 cup finely chopped onion

½ cup chopped green bell pepper

1 teaspoon red pepper flakes

1 (8-ounce) package sliced button mushrooms

3 garlic cloves, minced

1 tablespoon tomato paste

2 (8-ounce) cans tomato sauce

1 teaspoon dried oregano

½ teaspoon fennel seeds, crushed

1 (10-ounce) can refrigerated pizza crust dough, or Homemade Pizza Dough (page 194)

8 ounces fresh mozzarella cheese, sliced (about 6 slices)

4 ounces mozzarella cheese, shredded (1 cup)

1 cup grated Parmesan cheese

Chicago's best-loved food is deep-dish pizza. Do it up right, just as they do in the windy city, with heaping portions of spicy, hot Italian sausage, green peppers, fresh mushrooms, and onions. You can cheat a little and use refrigerated dough, but if you don't want to upset the mob, try making your own dough from scratch (see page 194).

Chicago-style pizza and our beloved home of Austin, Texas, have more of a connection than one might realize. Reportedly, the famous Chicago-style deep-dish pizza was invented by former University of Texas football star Ike Sewell. Go Horns!

1 Preheat the oven to 400°F. Lightly coat a 9 x 13-inch casserole dish with cooking spray.

2 Heat 2 teaspoons of the olive oil in a large nonstick skillet set over medium-high heat. Add the sausage, onion, bell pepper, and red pepper flakes to the pan and cook, breaking up any lumps with the back of a spoon, until the sausage is browned, about 8 minutes. Drain the sausage mixture, and set aside.

3 Return the pan to medium-high heat. Add the mushrooms and cook, stirring frequently, until the moisture evaporates, about 5 minutes. Transfer the mushrooms to a small bowl and set aside. Wipe the pan clean.

4 Return the pan to medium heat and add the remaining teaspoon of olive oil. Add the garlic and cook, stirring constantly until lightly browned. Add the tomato paste and cook, stirring frequently for 1 minute. Stir in the tomato

sauce, oregano, and fennel. Reduce the heat to low and simmer for 5 minutes or until the sauce is slightly thickened.

5 Unroll the pizza crust dough and press it into the bottom and halfway up the sides of the prepared casserole dish. Place a single layer of the mozzarella slices in the bottom of the pan to cover the dough (about 6 slices). Spoon the sausage mixture evenly over the cheese, then spoon the mushrooms over the sausage. Pour the sauce over the casserole and top with the shredded mozzarella and grated Parmesan cheeses.

6 Bake for 20 to 25 minutes or until the crust is browned and the cheeses bubble.

World's Greatest Chicken Pot Pie

MAKES 8 SERVINGS

2 tablespoons unsalted butter

1 (3-pound) roasted chicken, boned and shredded (see page 204)

¼ cup chopped red bell pepper

2 medium shallots, thinly sliced

3 tablespoons all-purpose flour

2 teaspoons salt

1 teaspoon dried tarragon, crushed

1 teaspoon freshly ground black pepper

2 cups whole milk

1 cup heavy cream

⅓ cup dry white wine

1½ cups fresh peas, blanched (see page 31)

1½ cups carrots, diced and blanched (see page 31)

2 russet potatoes, diced and blanched (see page 31)

1 sheet frozen puff pastry, thawed

Egg wash (lightly whisk together 1 whole egg and 1 teaspoon water)

It's called a defining moment. For Madonna, it was "Everybody." For Brad Pitt, it was *Thelma and Louise*. For us, well, it was our chicken pot pie that started it all. Now, we aren't saying that we're the next Madonna or Brad Pitt. But, in all honesty, you wouldn't be reading this book if it weren't for this recipe. As seen on Food Network's *Throwdown! with Bobby Flay,* this signature dish is our claim to fame. It's not just any old pot pie—oh, no. We took great care to bring this everyday comfort food to new gourmet heights. White wine, tarragon, and shallots are just some of the surprise ingredients tucked under a perfectly golden brown puff pastry. It's the dish that made people sit up and take notice of us, and now it's your turn to take the spotlight.

* * * * *

1 Preheat the oven to 425°F.

2 In a large skillet set over medium-high heat, melt the butter. Add the chicken, bell pepper, and shallots, and cook, stirring constantly, for 5 minutes. Stir in the flour, salt, tarragon, and black pepper. Add the milk and cream, and cook, stirring frequently, until the mixture is thick and bubbly, about 10 minutes. Add the wine, peas, carrots, and potatoes and stir until heated thoroughly, about 5 minutes.

3 Transfer the hot chicken mixture to a 9 x 13-inch casserole dish. Place the puff pastry over the top of the casserole dish. Brush the edges of the puff pastry with the egg wash and press against the side of the casserole dish, then cut slits in the pastry to allow steam to escape. Brush the top of the puff pastry with egg wash—this will help the puff pastry brown evenly. Bake for about 35 minutes or until the top is golden brown. Serve immediately.

Variations

Here are two other great ways to make our chicken pot pie:

Make individual pot pies! Portion out the filling into 6-ounce ramekins. Top each ramekin with some puff pastry and freeze. Cook at 425°F for 20 minutes or until puff pastry is golden brown. So cute!

Use store-bought pie dough and make empanadas! Using a 3-inch circle pastry cutter, cut 12 circles out of the dough. Place a large spoonful of filling on one half of each circle. Brush the edge of the pastry with egg wash, then fold in half to make a half-moon shape. Press the edges together firmly and crimp with a fork. Put the empanada on a baking sheet and bake at 350°F for about 30 minutes or until golden brown.

 Great for freezing! See our Freezer Tips on pages 23–27.

 Take advantage of frozen vegetables if you are short on time. Replace the hand-cut and blanched veggies with a bag of frozen peas and carrots and ½ bag of frozen diced potatoes. Our lips are sealed! Just make note that by not blanching your veggies you'll miss some of the salt flavor. Taste the filling before you put it in the casserole dish and season with salt, if you like.

Valley-Style Arroz con Pollo

MAKES 6 TO 8 SERVINGS

1 (3-pound) chicken, cut into 8 pieces, skin removed

2 teaspoons salt, plus more for chicken

2 teaspoons freshly ground black pepper, plus more for chicken

3 tablespoons olive oil

1 cup long-grain white rice

1 (14½-ounce) can diced tomatoes

1 (8-ounce) can tomato sauce

1 cup finely chopped onion

1 cup finely chopped green bell pepper

1 cup frozen peas

2 tablespoons tomato paste

3 garlic cloves, minced

3 bay leaves

2 teaspoons ground cumin

1 (32-ounce) carton chicken broth (see page 200), or as needed

"The Valley" is what we, in Texas, call the Rio Grande Valley. It's located on the southernmost tip of the state, bordering Mexico, and it's where Sandy grew up. The Valley is a melting pot of American and Mexican cultures, and is known for its festivals, architecture, and cuisine. So when Sandy talks about comfort food, she thinks of dishes that are often heavily influenced by traditional Mexican flavors. Arroz con Pollo (rice with chicken) is one of her favorites. Many Spanish-speaking countries claim this dish, so there are many different ways to prepare it. This particular recipe is served up Valley style and is uniquely Texan.

✳ ✳ ✳ ✳ ✳

1 Preheat the oven to 350°F.

2 Season the chicken with salt and pepper. Heat the olive oil in a large sauté pan set over high heat, and add 4 pieces of the chicken. Fry the chicken until browned, about 5 minutes on each side. Transfer the chicken to a paper towel–lined plate and set aside. In small batches, continue to fry the remaining pieces of chicken.

3 Add the rice to the oil remaining in the pan and fry over medium-high heat until it is golden brown, about 10 minutes. Add the tomatoes, tomato sauce, onion, bell pepper, peas, tomato paste, garlic, bay leaves, cumin, 2 teaspoons of salt, 2 teaspoons of black pepper, and 2½ cups of the broth. Bring to a boil, then transfer to a 9 x 13-inch casserole dish.

4 Add the chicken to the casserole dish, nestling the white meat into the rice to prevent it from overcooking, and place the dark meat on top of the rice. Cover the dish with foil and bake until the rice is tender and the chicken is no longer pink, 40 to 50 minutes. If needed, add more chicken broth, 1 cup at a time, to the dish during baking to keep the chicken and rice moist.

"Keep Austin Weird" Spam Casserole

MAKES 6 SERVINGS

2 pounds russet potatoes, thinly sliced

¼ teaspoon salt

Cooking spray

½ cup sliced onion

1 (12-ounce) can Spam

1 (10¾-ounce) can cream of celery soup

1 cup evaporated milk

¼ cup chopped green bell pepper

Paprika

Spam is alive and well here in Austin, Texas. (And oddly enough we do mean Austin, Texas, and not Austin, Minnesota, which happens to be the home of the Hormel product!) Since 1976, local Austinites have been celebrating this forgotten potted pork at the annual Spamarama Festival. The festival offers attendees a variety of options, such as the Spamalypics, the Spam Jam for local musicians, and our favorite competition, the Spam Cook-off! Here is a casserole dedicated to the beauty of Spam. We love you!

1 Preheat the oven to 350°F.

2 Put the potatoes in a saucepan with 2 cups of water and the salt. Cover the pan and set it over high heat. Bring to a boil and cook for 5 to 8 minutes. Drain well and set aside.

3 Lightly coat a 9 x 13-inch casserole dish with cooking spray. Put half of the potatoes in the bottom of the pan and cover with onion. Cut the Spam into 14 slices and layer 9 slices over the onion. Top with the remaining potatoes.

4 Combine the soup, milk, and green pepper, and pour over the casserole. Sprinkle with paprika and top the dish with the remaining 5 slices of Spam. Bake for about 45 minutes or until the potatoes are tender.

Tuna Noodle *Casserole*

Love it or hate it, the tuna noodle casserole is an American classic. This dish and the renowned green bean casserole are the two most asked about casseroles that are not currently on our menu. Why, you ask? We deliver our products frozen, and neither of these dishes freezes well. They're best when enjoyed fresh from the oven. With that said—and after the umpteenth request for this old-school favorite—we pay our respects here.

MAKES 8 SERVINGS

2 tablespoons unsalted butter

2 cups seasoned bread crumbs (see page 196)

1 (10-ounce) container sliced button mushrooms

1 medium onion, chopped

1½ teaspoons paprika

⅛ teaspoon cayenne

½ teaspoon salt, plus more for taste

3½ cups chicken broth (see page 200)

1 cup heavy cream

1 (8-ounce) package wide egg noodles

2 (6-ounce) cans water-packed solid white tuna, drained well and flaked

1½ cups frozen peas

2 cups grated Parmesan cheese (8 ounces)

2 tablespoons finely chopped fresh parsley leaves

Freshly ground black pepper

1 Preheat the oven to 475°F.

2 Melt 1 tablespoon of the butter in a large nonstick skillet set over medium-high heat. Add the bread crumbs and toast until just golden brown, 3 to 5 minutes. Transfer the crumbs to a small bowl and set aside.

3 Melt the remaining 1 tablespoon of butter in a medium sauté pan set over medium-high heat. Add the mushrooms, onion, paprika, cayenne, and ½ teaspoon salt and cook, stirring often, until the mushrooms and onion are golden brown, about 8 minutes. Stir in the broth and cream, and then add the noodles. Increase the heat to high and cook at a vigorous simmer, stirring often, until the noodles are nearly tender and the sauce is slightly thickened, about 8 minutes.

4 Remove the pan from the heat and stir in the tuna, peas, Parmesan, and parsley, and season to taste with salt and pepper. Pour the mixture into a 9 x 13-inch casserole dish and sprinkle the bread crumbs over the top. Bake until the edges are bubbly, about 8 minutes.

Don't get foiled by oil! Choose a solid white chunk tuna packed in water. Crystal found that oil-packed tuna can cause the casserole to be greasy.

Shrimply Delicious
Shrimp and Grits

MAKES 8 SERVINGS

Grits

Cooking spray

2 teaspoons unsalted butter

4 cups chopped sweet onions, such as Vidalia (about 2 large)

2 garlic cloves, minced

3 cups chicken broth (see page 200)

2 cups whole milk

½ teaspoon salt

1¼ cups quick-cooking grits

8 ounces smoked Gouda cheese, grated (2 cups)

2 large eggs, lightly beaten

¼ teaspoon freshly ground black pepper

Tomato Sauce

2 teaspoons olive oil

1 cup chopped sweet onion, such as a Vidalia

1½ cups chopped red bell peppers

1 tablespoon chopped fresh rosemary

2 (14½-ounce) cans Italian-flavored diced tomatoes

½ cup dry white wine

8 garlic cloves, minced

¼ teaspoon salt

Chances are, if you grew up in the South, you have eaten your fair share of grits. You've probably eaten your share of shrimp, too. It's no wonder that these two Southern staples come together in one of the best dishes of all time. Crystal grew up eating grits almost every morning and had always considered them a breakfast dish—until the day she was served shrimp and grits for dinner. That was when her obsession began. Instead of seeking help, Crystal continued to make shrimp and grits on her stove top, working and reworking the dish to find the perfect recipe. Her work definitely paid off. Here is her winning combo of smoked Gouda cheese grits and Cajun spiced shrimp, topped off with an herbed tomato mixture. Perfection indeed.

1 Preheat the oven to 375°F. Coat a 9 x 13-inch casserole dish with cooking spray.

2 For the grits, melt the butter in a large saucepan set over medium heat. Add the onions and garlic and cook for 8 minutes or until golden, stirring occasionally. Stir in the broth, milk, and salt and bring to a boil. Gradually add the grits, stirring constantly with a whisk. Reduce the heat to low, cover, and simmer for 5 minutes. Remove the pan from the heat; stir in the cheese, eggs, and pepper. Spoon the grits mixture into the prepared casserole dish. Bake for about 40 minutes or until firm.

3 For the tomato sauce, heat the oil in a large saucepan set over medium-high heat. Add the onion and sauté for 5 minutes. Add the bell pepper and rosemary and sauté for 1 minute. Stir in the tomatoes, wine, garlic, and salt. Bring

the mixture to a boil, reduce the heat to low, and simmer for 30 minutes.

4 For the shrimp, heat the oil in a nonstick skillet set over medium-high heat. In a small bowl, stir together the black pepper, white pepper, cayenne, paprika, onion powder, and garlic powder. Toss the shrimp in the seasoning mix, and then put the shrimp in the pan. Cook and stir for 3 minutes or until the shrimp are opaque.

5 To assemble the casserole, spread the tomato sauce over the grits in an even layer. Top the sauce with the shrimp. Serve immediately.

 Crystal grew up preparing shrimp for this dish. Here's how it's done: First, remove the shells and legs. Take a paring knife and make a shallow slit along the back of each shrimp. With the tip of the blade, lift up and remove the vein. The vein will tend to stick to your knife, so set a glass of water beside you while you work to dip your knife in and remove the vein before moving to the next shrimp.

Shrimp

2 teaspoons olive oil

1 teaspoon freshly ground black pepper

1 teaspoon ground white pepper

¼ teaspoon cayenne

1 teaspoon paprika

1 teaspoon onion powder

1 teaspoon garlic powder

1 pound large shrimp, peeled and deveined

Baked Four-Cheese Pasta

MAKES 8 TO 10 SERVINGS

Cooking spray

1 (16-ounce) box ziti or any other tube-shaped pasta

1 (14½-ounce) can diced tomatoes

3 tablespoons olive oil

1 cup chopped onion

12 garlic cloves, minced

⅔ cup dry white wine

2 cups heavy cream

1½ cups shredded Parmesan cheese (6 ounces)

1 cup crumbled Gorgonzola cheese (4 ounces)

2 cups mozzarella cheese, shredded (8 ounces)

1 cup shredded fontina cheese (4 ounces)

1 teaspoon salt

¾ teaspoon freshly ground black pepper

You haven't had a baked ziti like this before. Our version of this traditional favorite enhances the flavor with a creamy co-mingling of tangy Gorgonzola, nutty fontina, mozzarella, and sharp Parmesan cheese. Since this is such a rich and filling dish, it's great to serve when entertaining both vegetarians and meat lovers. Who doesn't love cheesy baked pasta?

If you can't find Gorgonzola or fontina at your local market, you can substitute! Use regular ol' blue cheese for the Gorgonzola and replace the fontina with shredded Italian cheese mix. These prepared cheese mixes usually include a variety of tasty Italian cheeses that complement this dish perfectly.

✳ ✳ ✳ ✳ ✳

1 Preheat the oven to 425°F. Lightly coat a 9 x 13-inch casserole dish with cooking spray.

2 Cook the pasta according to the package directions. Drain the pasta and put it in the prepared casserole dish. Stir in the tomatoes and their juices. Set aside.

3 Heat the oil in a large saucepan set over medium-high heat. Add the onion and garlic and cook until just soft, about 8 minutes. Add the wine and cook for about 4 more minutes or until the liquid is reduced by half. Reduce the heat to medium and add the cream. Simmer gently, stirring frequently, for about 5 minutes or until the mixture starts to thicken slightly. Remove the pan from the heat. Stir in the Parmesan, Gorgonzola, mozzarella, and fontina cheeses, and season with salt and pepper.

4 Pour the cheese mixture over the pasta. Cover the pan with foil and bake for 30 to 35 minutes or until the sauce is bubbly. Remove from the oven and stir to make sure the cheese and pasta are thoroughly combined.

 Great for freezing! See our Freezer Tips on pages 23–27.

 Vegetarian friendly!

End up with extra Gorgonzola? Put it to good use! Sandy loves to stuff it into a fresh fig, then wrap the fig in a very thin slice of prosciutto. Voilà! A sophisticated garnish for a salad or an easy appetizer for your next cocktail party.

Mamaw's Stuffed Peppers

MAKES 6 SERVINGS

6 green bell peppers

1 pound ground beef

1 large onion, finely chopped

2 garlic cloves, minced

1 teaspoon salt

¼ teaspoon freshly ground black pepper

2 (14¾-ounce) cans diced tomatoes

1 teaspoon Worcestershire sauce

½ teaspoon ground allspice

1 cup cooked long-grain white rice (see page 195)

Cooking spray

1 tablespoon unsalted butter

½ cup seasoned bread crumbs (see page 196)

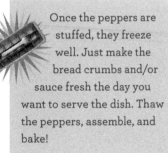
Once the peppers are stuffed, they freeze well. Just make the bread crumbs and/or sauce fresh the day you want to serve the dish. Thaw the peppers, assemble, and bake!

Crystal's "Mamaw" Cook served these delicious stuffed peppers with a delectable buttered bread-crumb topping. These bad boys are sauce-free, and preferred that way so that the taste of the pepper comes through. But neither Crystal nor Mamaw Cook will take offense if you want to add a little sauce. (See opposite for a tomato sauce that's a great match for this dish.)

1 Preheat the oven to 350°F.

2 Cut off the top of each bell pepper and remove the seeds. Put the peppers in a large pot of boiling salted water and cook for 5 minutes. Drain well and set aside.

3 Set a skillet over medium heat. Add the beef, onion, and garlic, and season with salt and pepper. Cook, breaking up any lumps with the back of a spoon, until the beef is browned thoroughly, about 10 minutes. Add the tomatoes and simmer for 10 minutes. Add the Worcestershire sauce, allspice, and rice; stir well.

4 Coat a 9 x 13-inch casserole dish with cooking spray. Stuff the peppers with beef mixture and place them in the prepared casserole dish. In a small saucepan, melt the butter. Remove the pan from the heat and stir in the bread crumbs. Scatter the bread crumbs over the peppers and place the dish in the oven. Bake for 25 minutes or until the bread crumbs are golden brown and the meat is heated thoroughly.

Mary Ann's Favorite Tomato Sauce

Crystal's Aunt Mary Ann prefers to accompany her stuffed peppers with a rich tomato sauce.

MAKES 4 CUPS

2 tablespoons unsalted butter

1 medium onion, diced

2 garlic cloves, minced

3 cups diced canned tomatoes

1/2 cup finely minced celery

1 1/2 tablespoons white wine vinegar

1 tablespoon minced fresh parsley

1 teaspoon sugar

1 1/2 teaspoons salt

1/2 teaspoon freshly ground black pepper

In a saucepan set over low heat, melt the butter. Add the onion and garlic; sauté for about 8 minutes or until tender. Add the tomatoes, celery, vinegar, parsley, sugar, salt, and pepper and cook about 10 minutes. Pour the sauce over the peppers before baking.

Here's a tip from Crystal for keeping stuffed peppers upright in the oven. When you remove the pepper tops to insert the stuffing, don't throw them away! Instead, put the tops between the stuffed peppers for extra stability.

Easy Eggplant Parmesan

MAKES 6 SERVINGS

1 large eggplant, cut into
6 to 8 slices

1 teaspoon salt, plus more for
the eggplant

⅓ cup plus 2 tablespoons
olive oil

1 medium yellow onion, chopped

2 garlic cloves, minced

1 (14½-ounce) can diced
tomatoes

1 (15-ounce) can tomato sauce

1 (6-ounce) can tomato paste

2 teaspoons dried oregano

1 teaspoon dried basil

¼ teaspoon dried rosemary,
crushed

1 teaspoon sugar

½ teaspoon freshly ground
black pepper

Pinch of ground cinnamon

Cooking spray

⅓ cup grated Parmesan cheese
(1½ ounces)

2 tablespoons all-purpose flour

2 tablespoons seasoned bread
crumbs (see page 196)

1 large egg

8 ounces mozzarella cheese,
shredded (2 cups)

Crystal's sister, Cindy, has always been a fantastic cook, but recently she has found a special connection in the kitchen. During a year-and-a-half-long treatment for breast cancer, she found that cooking is amazing therapy. Not only has Cindy been a great sounding board for our recipes, she concocted this easy, nutritious, and delicious dish that is so tasty that we just had to share it with the rest of the world. Go Cindy! Go Cindy!

1 Lay the eggplant slices on a wire rack that is nestled in a baking pan. Generously sprinkle the eggplant with salt and let them sit for up to 1 hour. Rinse the eggplant slices under cold water to remove the salt, then pat dry.

2 Heat 2 tablespoons of the olive oil in a large sauté pan or saucepan set over medium heat. Add the onion and garlic, and sauté until soft, about 8 minutes. Add the tomatoes, tomato sauce, and tomato paste, stirring until well blended. Add the oregano, basil, rosemary, sugar, 1 teaspoon salt, pepper, and cinnamon. Simmer for 20 to 30 minutes.

3 Meanwhile, preheat the oven to 350°F. Lightly coat a 9 x 13-inch casserole dish with cooking spray.

4 Combine the Parmesan, flour, and bread crumbs in a plate or other shallow dish. In a small bowl, beat the egg with 1 tablespoon of water.

5 Heat the remaining ⅓ cup olive oil in a large skillet set over medium heat. Dip each eggplant slice into the egg, shaking off the excess. Press the slices into the cheese mixture, coating both sides. Working in batches, put the

slices in the hot oil and cook until crisp and golden brown, 2 to 3 minutes each side. Transfer the eggplant to a paper towel-lined plate and let drain. Repeat with the remaining eggplant slices.

6 Arrange the eggplant slices in the bottom of the prepared casserole dish. Sprinkle the eggplant slices with half of the mozzarella. Top with the tomato mixture, and sprinkle with the remaining mozzarella. (Top with an additional dusting of Parmesan cheese, if desired.) Bake for approximately 25 minutes, until the sauce is bubbling. Allow to stand for 5 minutes before serving.

Vegetarian friendly!

Jayne's Baked Spaghetti

MAKES 10 SERVINGS

1 (16-ounce) package angel hair pasta

Cooking spray

2 tablespoons unsalted butter

1 cup chopped onion

1 cup chopped celery

1 (28-ounce) can diced tomatoes

1 (4-ounce) can sliced button mushrooms, drained

1 (2¼-ounce) can sliced black olives, drained

2 teaspoons dried oregano

8 ounces Cheddar cheese, shredded (2 cups)

1 (10¾-ounce) can cream of mushroom soup, or 1½ cups homemade Cream of Mushroom Soup (page 203)

¼ cup whole milk

¼ ounce grated Parmesan cheese

Every family has a signature dish, and this one belongs to the Lovitt family. Sandy's other half, Michael, grew up on this dish, and to this day his mom makes it for him whenever he goes home to visit. In fact, Michael's mom, Jayne, has been making this dish ever since she was newly wed to her husband, Mike. The story goes that when Jayne and Mike were first married, they spent a lot of time with another couple in the neighborhood (we'll call them "Bob and Sally"). Jayne, Mike, Bob, and Sally would get together on a regular basis and play cards. Eventually, they decided that they would start making dinner for each other, too. This tradition didn't last long before Bob called and said they could no longer participate in the dinner parties. When Jayne asked if everything was okay, Bob said that Sally was *very* upset because there was no way she could ever compete with Jayne's baked spaghetti. They haven't spoken in thirty years!

1 Cook the pasta according to the package directions. Set aside.

2 Preheat the oven to 350°F. Lightly coat a 9 x 13-inch casserole dish with cooking spray.

3 In a large sauté pan set over medium heat, melt the butter. Add the onion and celery and cook until tender, about 8 minutes. Add the tomatoes, mushrooms, olives, and oregano. Reduce the heat to low and cook for 10 minutes.

4 In the prepared casserole dish, layer half of the pasta, half of the sauce, and half of the Cheddar cheese. Repeat the layers with the remaining ingredients.

5 Combine the soup and milk, stirring until smooth, and pour over the top of the casserole. Sprinkle with the Parmesan cheese and bake for 30 to 40 minutes or until the pasta is bubbling around the edges.

Vegetarian friendly!

Variation

A simple way to enrich this dish is to add beef. Season 1 pound of ground beef with salt and freshly ground black pepper, and brown it in a large sauté pan set over medium-high heat. Add the meat to the sauce while it simmers so that the flavors have time to marry.

The Savory Gourmet

Whether you're planning a weekend dinner party, a special occasion with your sweetheart, or a holiday gathering, there's a recipe in this chapter for you. These dishes may take a little more time and effort, or call for more than your everyday ingredients, but we'll guide you through them and you'll have fun at the same time.

As mentioned, we sought to use ingredients for these recipes not typically found in staple casseroles, such as buttery lobster, tender lamb, and fresh crab. Those with more sophisticated palates will be delighted that the humble casserole can meet their gourmet expectations. And the best part? These are still make-ahead dishes, which means more party time with your guests.

Osso Bucco

Beef Burgundy

Greek Pastitsio

Charlotte's Prime Rib

Curry Cure-All Chicken
Casserole

Chicken Penne Pasta
with Pink Sauce

Chicken Divan Crêpes with Gruyère

Coq au Vin

Pimpin' Paella

Boo-yah Bouillabaisse

Seafood Lasagna Rolls
with Panko Crumb Topping

Halibut Enchiladas with
Salsa Verde

Shrimp with Seared Polenta

Savory Salmon Turnovers

Lobster Boy Casserole

Asparagus and Crab Casserole

Crawfish Casserole

Osso Bucco
Fit for a Queen!

MAKES 6 SERVINGS

¼ cup all-purpose flour

Salt and freshly ground black pepper

6 (½-pound each) veal shanks or lamb shanks

½ cup vegetable oil

¼ cup (½ stick) unsalted butter

1 cup chopped carrots

1 cup chopped celery

1 cup chopped onion

4 garlic cloves, minced

3 fresh thyme sprigs

2 bay leaves

1 fresh rosemary sprig

1½ cups dry white wine

1 tablespoon tomato paste

3 cups veal stock or chicken broth (see page 200), plus more as needed

1 (14½-ounce) can diced tomatoes

4 tablespoons chopped fresh flat-leaf parsley

1 tablespoon grated lemon zest

Put some lovin' in your oven! This fabulous dish gets its rich flavor from slowly brazing the veal until the meat is so tender, it literally falls off the bone with the touch of your fork. As it cooks, the aromas of the fresh herbs, earthy vegetables, and wine fill the kitchen. In fact, you may have to keep yourself busy by reading this cookbook until the timer goes off, lest you dig in before it's done. Seriously, if you have never tried osso bucco, this is your chance! It takes a little more time—and expense—to cook than other dishes, but it's completely worth it. Traditionally osso bucco is served over risotto, but we like it best over a bed of mashed potatoes or cooked white rice. So go ahead and treat yourself, you deserve it. If you're not keen on veal, you can use lamb instead.

1 Preheat the oven to 325°F.

2 Put the flour on a plate and season it with salt and pepper. Pat the shanks dry with paper towels. Dredge each shank in the seasoned flour, making sure to shake off any excess flour. Heat the vegetable oil in a heavy Dutch oven or large sauté pan set over high heat until just smoking. Working in batches so as not to crowd the pan, place shanks in the oil in a single layer. Cook the shanks until browned on each side, about 4 minutes per side. Remove the shanks from the pan and set aside.

3 Reduce the heat to medium high, then add the butter, carrots, celery, and onion to the pan and sauté for about 8 minutes or until the vegetables begin to soften. Add the garlic and sauté for 2 more minutes.

4 Meanwhile, make a bouquet garni: place the thyme, bay leaves, and rosemary on a square of cheesecloth, gather

the corners at the top, and tie the cloth closed with some kitchen twine. Add the bouquet garni to the sautéed vegetables. Increase the heat to high and add the wine. Bring the mixture to a boil and cook, making sure to scrape up the browned bits at the bottom of the pan, until the liquid is reduced by about half, about 10 minutes. Add the tomato paste and stir to combine.

5 Return the shanks to the pan and add the stock and diced tomatoes. Cover the pan and place it in the oven. Now, go make yourself a cocktail and wait. This dish will need to braise for 1½ to 2 hours or until the meat is super-tender and falling off the bone. Check on it occasionally to make sure there's enough liquid in the pan. The shanks should be submerged in liquid by about three-fourths of the way up the shank. If the pan dries out some, just add more stock. Flip the shanks a couple of times during cooking so that both sides sit in the amazing juice for a while.

6 The meat is done when it is falling off the bone. Transfer the shanks to a serving platter. Remove the bouquet garni and discard. Spoon the liquid from the pan over the shanks and sprinkle with the parsley and lemon zest.

Sandy's first restaurant job out of culinary school was at a locally owned restaurant here in Austin called Jeffrey's. This restaurant has a fabulous reputation and Sandy was lucky enough to work with amazing chefs who inspired and challenged her in the kitchen and taught her many invaluable lessons. One of her most vivid memories of working there was the excitement around the addition of osso bucco to their menu each fall. Rich and decadent, it was only around for a limited time. Our osso bucco recipe is a nod to the talented crew at Jeffrey's.

Beef Burgundy

MAKES 8 SERVINGS

8 slices bacon, chopped

3 pounds stew meat or boneless beef chuck, cut into ¾-inch cubes

Salt

⅛ teaspoon freshly ground black pepper, plus more for beef

⅓ cup all-purpose flour

2 yellow onions, chopped

1 pound carrots, peeled and cut into 1-inch pieces

1 pound sliced button mushrooms

5 large garlic cloves, minced

3½ cups beef broth (see page 201)

1 bottle dry red wine, preferably Burgundy

⅓ cup chopped fresh thyme leaves

1 tablespoon firmly packed light brown sugar

1 tablespoon tomato paste

1 bay leaf

This delicious, classic dish from the Burgundy region of France is designed to showcase the wines for which the area is famous. (We like anything that celebrates wine. *Oui, oui!*) Beef Burgundy can appear at first glance as a mere stew, but those of us who have had the pleasure of making this dish know that during the hours it slowly cooks in the oven something magical happens. The flavors of the broth are intensified by the wine, and it thickens into a velvety smooth sauce. Once finished, the cuts of beef are so tender they almost seem to melt. Traditionally, Beef Burgundy is made with wine from the French province of Burgundy. If you have trouble finding a true Burgundy (they can be pretty pricy!), the best substitutes are Pinot Noirs from California or Oregon. We suggest serving this over our Perfect Rice Every Time (page 195) and with our Rockin' Tomatoes Rockefeller (page 139).

✳ ✳ ✳ ✳ ✳

1 Preheat the oven to 350°F.

2 Cook the bacon in a heavy ovenproof Dutch oven set over high heat until crisp, about 7 minutes. Transfer the bacon to a paper towel–lined plate. Set aside.

3 Season the beef generously with salt and pepper, and toss in the flour. Working in three batches so as not to crowd the pot, add the meat to the pot with the rendered bacon fat. Cook the beef, turning to brown all sides, about 5 minutes per batch. Transfer the meat to a large bowl.

4 Into the same pot, add the onions, carrots, mushrooms, and ⅛ teaspoon of the pepper and cook until the vegetables are light brown, about 8 minutes. Add the garlic and sauté for 1 minute. Transfer the vegetables to the bowl with the beef.

5 Add 1½ cups of the broth to the pot. Bring to a boil and cook, scraping up browned bits on the bottom of the pan, until reduced to a glaze, about 8 minutes.

6 Return the meat and vegetables and their juices to the pot. Add the wine, thyme, brown sugar, tomato paste, bay leaf, and the remaining 2 cups of broth. Bring to a boil, stirring occasionally. Cover the pot and place it in the oven. Braise until the beef is tender, about 2 hours. Remove the bay leaf before serving.

When it comes to cooking with wine, Sandy follows the sage advice of Julia Child, who said, "If you do not have a good wine to use, it is far better to omit it, for a poor one can spoil a simple dish and utterly debase a noble one."

Greek Pastitsio

MAKES 8 TO 10 SERVINGS

1 (16-ounce) package dried macaroni

1½ cups (3 sticks) unsalted butter, melted

2 cups whole milk

6 large eggs, beaten

8 ounces mizithra cheese, shredded, or romano cheese, grated (2 cups)

8 ounces feta cheese, crumbled (2 cups)

¾ cup grated Parmesan cheese (3 ounces)

¼ teaspoon grated nutmeg

1 teaspoon ground white pepper

1½ pounds ground beef

Salt and freshly ground black pepper

3 tablespoons olive oil

1 medium onion, chopped

1 garlic clove, minced

1 (6-ounce) can tomato paste

½ cup dry red wine

½ cup beef broth (see page 201)

2 tablespoons chopped fresh parsley

½ teaspoon sugar

10 sheets frozen phyllo pastry, thawed

This Greek casserole is traditionally pasta baked in a flavorful meat sauce and topped with another sauce, such as béchamel. But we decided to skip the extra layer of sauce and cover ours with layers of buttery, flaky phyllo dough instead. The phyllo adds a nice crunch to this delicious dish, making a truly scrumptious, savory pie. Don't pull out your best dinnerware for this one. It's so tasty, you'll want to throw your plate and yell "Opa"!

Note that the cheeses won't really melt. They will soften and become nice and creamy, but it won't be gooey like a Cheddar or American cheese.

✳ ✳ ✳ ✳ ✳

1 Preheat the oven to 350°F.

2 Cook the macaroni according to the package directions and drain well. Return the cooked macaroni to the pot and add 1 cup of the melted butter, the milk, eggs, mizithra, feta, and Parmesan cheeses, nutmeg, and white pepper. Stir until well combined. Pour the macaroni mixture into a 9 x 13-inch casserole dish.

3 Heat a large skillet over medium-high heat. Add the ground beef, season with salt and pepper, and cook, stirring until browned thoroughly, about 10 minutes. Drain well and set meat aside. Return the skillet to medium-high heat and add the oil, onion, and garlic. Sauté until soft, about 8 minutes. Return the meat to the pan and add the tomato paste, red wine, beef broth, parsley, sugar, and salt and pepper to taste. Cover and simmer for 20 minutes. Remove the pan from the heat and let cool for 5 minutes. Pour over the macaroni mixture. Place one sheet of the phyllo on top of the macaroni. Using a pastry brush and the remaining ½ cup of melted butter, lightly coat the phyllo with butter.

Working quickly, add another sheet of phyllo and brush it with butter. Repeat the layers until you have used all 10 sheets of phyllo. (You may need to overlap the phyllo sheets to entirely cover the pasta.) Cut two or three vents in the top of the pastry.

4 Bake for 45 to 55 minutes, or until the pastry is golden brown and the eggs and cheese are set. Cool the casserole slightly before cutting into squares and serving.

Though working with phyllo dough takes a little extra work, Crystal is always thrilled with the results we get. So light and flaky, it makes a tasty topping for many casseroles and pastry dishes. We always work with frozen sheets of phyllo (it's inexpensive and awesome) and find that it is easiest to use when thawed in the refrigerator overnight.

Here are a few of Crystal's tips for working with this delicate dough. Have a few things on hand when you start to layer the sheets: a pastry brush, a small bowl of melted butter, damp paper towels, and parchment paper. To get started, remove the pastry sheets from the package and unfold them onto parchment paper. Cover the dough with damp paper towels to keep the pastry moist. (Phyllo dries out quickly, so it's important to keep the dough covered.) Work with one sheet at a time, keeping the rest covered.

You can store the sheets in the refrigerator for up to three days, wrapped well in foil, but do not try to refreeze any sheets that have been thawed. Unused packages can be stored in the freezer for up to a couple of months.

Charlotte's Prime Rib

MAKES 6 TO 8 SERVINGS

1 (5-pound) rib roast, bone-in

2 garlic cloves, quartered

2 (10½-ounce) cans beef consommé

2 tablespoons Lawry's seasoned salt

Freshly ground black pepper

2 (14½-ounce) cans chopped tomatoes

2 medium onions, quartered

2 celery ribs, roughly chopped

2 bay leaves

2 tablespoons Worcestershire sauce

Crystal's mom, Charlotte, should have installed a revolving door in their home, as it was the place where everyone stopped by—conveniently right around dinnertime. Charlotte fed almost everyone in Blue Ridge—the small town located in the North Georgia Mountains where Crystal grew up—for years and finally decided to make a successful catering business of it. Her prime rib was by far one of the most requested items and has become a Cook family holiday favorite. Lucky for Charlotte, her recipe made it into this book, so now she can stop by someone else's house for dinner.

✳ ✳ ✳ ✳ ✳

1 Preheat the oven to 375°F.

2 Make 8 slits in top of the roast and stuff each with a garlic piece. Place the roast in a roasting pan and cover with the consommé, seasoned salt, pepper, tomatoes, onions, celery, and bay leaves. Cover with foil and bake for about 1 hour. Remove roast from pan, let rest 10 minutes, then wrap tightly with plastic wrap and place in refrigerator overnight. Place the pan juices in a covered container and refrigerate overnight.

3 The next day, remove the container of pan juice from the refrigerator, skim the grease from the top of the juice, strain out the vegetables, and add the Worcestershire sauce. Unwrap the meat and put the roast and juices into a 9 x 13-inch casserole dish and roast the meat again for 30 minutes or until the internal temperature reaches 130°F (medium-rare).

Curry Cure-All Chicken Casserole

When sick, people typically head straight for chicken noodle soup or some other mild-flavored, broth-based soup to nurse them back to health. Not Crystal. Oddly enough, when Crystal is feeling a little under the weather, she craves spice to comfort her. We're talking hot-and-sour soup, pho with lots of Sriracha sauce, and her ultimate cure-all favorite, curry! Extremely satisfying, this dish's fragrant spices alone will perk you right up. Serve over steamed jasmine rice or with traditional Indian bread called naan.

MAKES 6 SERVINGS

4 tablespoons olive oil

1 large onion, chopped

½ red bell pepper, chopped

4 garlic cloves, minced

5 teaspoons curry powder

1 teaspoon salt

6 boneless, skinless chicken breasts, cut into 1-inch pieces

5 medium russet potatoes, peeled and dried

3 cups chicken broth (see page 200)

1 Preheat the oven to 350°F.

2 In a large saucepan set over medium heat, heat the oil. Add the onion, bell pepper, garlic, curry powder, and salt, and sauté for about 8 minutes. Watch this step closely since the garlic and curry powder can burn easily if left unattended. Using a slotted spoon, remove the vegetables from the pan and set them aside.

3 Add the chicken to the pan and sauté for 8 minutes or until almost cooked. If the pan gets dry, add a little more oil. Add the potatoes and onion mixture to the saucepan and stir well. Pour the curry into a 9 x 13-inch casserole dish. Pour the chicken stock into the dish until the curry is just covered.

4 Bake for about 45 minutes or until the sauce starts to thicken to a gravy-like consistency and the potatoes are tender.

Chicken Penne Pasta with Pink Sauce

MAKES 6 TO 8 SERVINGS

6 ounces dried penne pasta

3 boneless, skinless whole chicken breasts

2 tablespoons olive oil

Salt and freshly ground black pepper

Cooking spray

2 garlic cloves, minced

1 cup coarsely chopped prosciutto

½ medium green bell pepper, cut into 1 x ¼-inch strips

½ medium yellow bell pepper, cut into 1 x ¼-inch strips

3 tablespoons drained capers

1 teaspoon dried basil, crushed

1 (15-ounce) jar marinara sauce, or 2 cups homemade Marinara Sauce (page 199)

1 (10-ounce) jar Alfredo sauce

⅓ cup grated Parmesan cheese (1½ ounces)

Tomato or cream sauce? Who says you have to choose? This casserole combines marinara and Alfredo sauces to create a lovely pink sauce. The cream balances the acidity of the tomatoes, while sophisticated ingredients such as prosciutto and capers add an inviting gourmet touch to the meal. This recipe is perfect for Valentine's Day, first dates, or anniversaries. Not only will there be a pleasing blush to your meal, but perhaps to your sweetie, too!

1 Cook the pasta according to the package directions and drain well. Return the pasta to the pot and set aside.

2 Coat the chicken breasts with 1 tablespoon of the olive oil and season with salt and pepper. Place the chicken on a baking sheet lined with foil and bake for 15 to 20 minutes or until cooked through. Remove the pan from the oven and let the chicken cool. When it is cool enough to handle, dice the chicken and set it aside.

3 Preheat the oven to 350°F. Coat a 9 x 13-inch casserole dish with cooking spray.

4 In a large skillet set over medium-high heat, heat the remaining 1 tablespoon of olive oil. Add the cooked chicken and the garlic, and cook, stirring, for 2 minutes. Add the prosciutto, green and yellow peppers, capers, and basil. Cook, stirring frequently, for 2 to 3 minutes or until the peppers just start to soften. Add the chicken mixture to the reserved penne and mix well. Spread half of the mixture in a 9 x 13-inch casserole dish coated with cooking spray.

5 In a medium bowl, combine the marinara and Alfredo sauces. Ta-da! Pink sauce! Top the penne with 1 cup of the pink sauce. Put the remaining penne mixture over the sauce, then add the remaining pink sauce. Sprinkle the top with Parmesan cheese. Bake for 25 to 30 minutes or until the cheese is melted and slightly browned and the casserole is heated through. Remove the pan from the oven and toss the pasta thoroughly

Crystal found a clever way to make peeling garlic a snap. Zap the garlic cloves in the microwave for 15 seconds and the peels will slide right off.

Chicken Divan Crêpes with Gruyère

MAKES 10 SERVINGS

1 head of broccoli, cut into florets, or 1 (10-ounce) package frozen chopped broccoli, defrosted and drained well

1 (3-pound) roasted chicken, boned and shredded (see page 204)

1 (10¾-ounce) can cream of mushroom soup, or 1½ cups homemade Cream of Mushroom Soup (page 203)

8 ounces Gruyère cheese, grated (2 cups)

½ cup mayonnaise

½ cup sour cream

¼ cup dry white wine

1½ teaspoons fresh lemon juice

½ teaspoon curry powder

Salt and freshly ground black pepper

1 (4.5-ounce) package prepared crêpes (10 crêpes), or homemade (recipe follows)

Cooking spray

1 cup grated Parmesan cheese (4 ounces)

½ cup seasoned bread crumbs (see page 196)

2 tablespoons unsalted butter, melted

Aunt Joan. Crystal's aunt oozed charm and elegance. She always wore just the right dress or scarf. She was rarely without beautiful makeup and glam sunglasses. Her table was always set perfectly, and it was filled with foods that, for her young nieces, seemed exotic but tasty and comforting at the same time. The young ladies in Crystal's family all grew up aspiring to be as lovely and sophisticated as Aunt Joan. We have modified Aunt Joan's recipe for chicken divan by using it as a filling for crêpes. This recipe honors the beautiful and loving woman who graced so many lives and created so many special meals. Enjoy!

✳ ✳ ✳ ✳ ✳

1 Preheat the oven to 350°F.

2 If working with fresh broccoli, steam the florets for 3 to 5 minutes. Drain well and put broccoli into a large mixing bowl. Add the chicken to the bowl, stir well, and set aside.

3 In a large bowl, combine the soup, cheese, mayonnaise, sour cream, wine, lemon juice, curry powder, salt, and pepper. Add half the soup mixture to the broccoli and chicken and stir well.

4 Lay the crêpes on a cutting board. Divide the chicken filling among the 10 crêpes, then roll them up. Lightly coat two 9 x 13-inch casserole dishes with cooking spray. Divide the crêpes between the two casserole dishes, placing the crêpes seem side down. Spread the remaining soup mixture over the crêpes. Combine the Parmesan, bread crumbs, and butter in a small bowl, and sprinkle over the tops of the crêpes. Bake until bubbly, 25 to 30 minutes.

Homemade Crêpes

We save time in this recipe by using ready-made crêpes. But if you have the extra time to make your own, you will only enhance your results. If working with crêpes is something you've never done, double the batter and give yourself plenty of time for a practice run!

1 In a large bowl, whisk together the flour and the eggs. Add the milk and whisk together. Add the salt, curry powder, and butter; whisk until smooth.

2 Lightly grease a medium skillet with cooking spray and set over medium-high heat. Pour ¼ cup of the batter into the pan. Working quickly, tilt the pan in all directions to coat the entire bottom surface of the pan with the batter. Let the crêpe cook until lightly browned, about 2 minutes. Flip the crêpe and cook the second side until lightly browned, about 1 more minute. Repeat with the remaining batter.

MAKES 10 TO 12 CRÊPES

1½ cups all-purpose flour

3 large eggs

1½ cups whole milk

½ teaspoon salt

⅛ teaspoon curry powder (optional)

4 tablespoons (½ stick) unsalted butter, melted

Cooking spray

Coq  au Vin

MAKES 6 SERVINGS

4 slices bacon, chopped

½ cup chopped onion

1 (3-pound) chicken, cut into 8 pieces

8 shallots, thinly sliced

1 carrot, coarsely chopped

2 garlic cloves, minced

3 tablespoons cognac

2 tablespoons unsalted butter

1 (10-ounce) container sliced button mushrooms

4 flat-leaf parsley sprigs

2 bay leaves

2 fresh thyme sprigs

1 celery rib, coarsely chopped

2 cups dry red wine, such as Pinot Noir

The Queens go "coo-coo" for Coq au Vin, a classic French dish of chicken cooked in red wine. An elegant but simple recipe, it's a great entry point to the world of French cuisine, which is often less complicated than it seems. Since this chicken dish has a decadent sauce, we love serving it in a shallow soup bowl over buttered egg noodles that have been tossed with chopped fresh parsley. We also garnish the rest of the plate with parsley, as the bright green pops against the red wine sauce. So pretty and so tasty!

1 Preheat the oven to 350°F.

2 In large sauté pan set over medium heat, cook the bacon and onion until the bacon is crisp and the onion is translucent, about 8 minutes. Transfer the bacon and onion to a plate, leaving the rendered fat in the pan. Add the chicken to the pan and cook, turning, until browned on all sides, about 10 minutes. Remove the chicken from the pan and set aside. Add the shallots, carrot, garlic, and cognac to the pan and cook, stirring, for 3 minutes.

3 In a separate small sauté pan set over medium heat, melt the butter and sauté the mushrooms until slightly browned, about 5 minutes. Set aside.

4 Make a bouquet garni by wrapping the parsley, bay leaves, and thyme in cheesecloth and tying the cloth closed with kitchen twine. Place the bouquet garni in the bottom of a 9 x 13-inch casserole dish. Add the chicken, vegetables, and mushrooms to the casserole dish.

5 Pour the wine into the sauté pan used to cook the chicken, set over high heat, and bring to a boil, using a wooden spoon to scrape up the brown bits from the bottom of the pan. Pour the wine over the chicken in the casserole dish. Cover the dish with foil and bake for 2 hours or until the chicken juices run clear when the meat is pierced. Remove the bouquet garni and serve.

This dish makes for an elegant presentation and is perfect for dinner guests. Consider making it a day ahead, so that the flavors can further meld together—and give yourself some extra time to enjoy your company! Just prepare the recipe up to the point before baking, cover, and store in the fridge. Now all you have to do the day your guests come is preheat your oven and create a mouthwatering aroma for your guests to enjoy as the dish bakes. Yep, it is that easy.

Pimpin' Paella

MAKES 8 SERVINGS

1 tablespoon olive oil

5 slices bacon, chopped

1 (3½-pound) chicken, cut into 8 pieces

Salt and freshly ground black pepper

2 cups chopped onions (2 large)

4 garlic cloves, minced

2 cups long-grain white rice

1 (7-ounce) jar roasted sliced pimientos with juice

½ teaspoon crushed saffron threads

2 cups bottled clam juice

1½ cups chicken broth (page 200)

1 pound fresh large shrimp, peeled and deveined

1 pound cleaned fresh squid, cut into ½-inch rings

1 dozen clams, scrubbed

1 dozen mussels, scrubbed and debearded

1 cup frozen green peas, thawed

Lemon wedges

No special equipment needed here. Leave the paella pan at the store and let your casserole dish do the work. Packed with fresh seafood and accentuated with the alluring flavor of saffron, your kids may call this pimpin' dish "The Bomb," which means it's good.

This dish lives or dies by the freshness of the fish. The beauty of paella is that it is a flexible dish, so talk to your local fishmonger to get recommendations on the best catch of the day. If you don't like seafood, the dish actually works really well without it, too.

1 Preheat the oven to 450°F.

2 Heat the olive oil in a heavy, ovenproof Dutch oven over medium heat. Add the bacon and cook until crisp and the fat is rendered, about 6 minutes. Using a slotted spoon, transfer the bacon to a paper towel–lined plate to drain. Set aside.

3 Sprinkle the chicken pieces with salt and pepper. Add the chicken to the bacon drippings in the Dutch oven and cook over medium heat until browned on all sides, about 7 minutes per piece. Remove the chicken from the pot and set aside.

4 Add the onions and garlic to the Dutch oven and sauté until they just begin to brown, scraping up any browned bits as you go, about 8 minutes. Stir in the rice, pimientos with their juice, and saffron. Add the clam juice and chicken broth, and bring mixture to a simmer. Remove the pot from the heat.

5 Nestle the chicken, shrimp, squid, clams, and mussels into the rice mixture. Sprinkle with the bacon and peas, and cover the pot.

6 Bake the paella until the chicken is cooked through, the clams and mussels open, and the rice is tender, 25 to 30 minutes (discard any clams and mussels that do not open). Uncover the Dutch oven and let the paella stand for 10 minutes. Serve with the lemon wedges on the side.

 Crystal was fascinated to learn that it takes 225,000 handpicked saffron stigmas to make a single pound, which explains why it's the world's most expensive spice—around $2,700 per pound!

Boo-yah Bouillabaisse

MAKES 8 SERVINGS

¼ cup (½ stick) unsalted butter

1 medium yellow onion, chopped

1 red bell pepper, chopped

6 garlic cloves, minced

1 (46-ounce) can tomato juice

1 large tomato, chopped

3 tablespoons all-purpose flour

1 tablespoon packed light brown sugar

1 tablespoon Sriracha hot sauce

2 teaspoons grated orange zest

1 teaspoon curry powder

¾ teaspoon dried thyme

¼ teaspoon saffron threads

2 teaspoons salt

1 teaspoon freshly ground black pepper

½ cup dry white wine

3 tablespoons fresh lemon juice

¼ cup plus 2 tablespoons chopped fresh parsley

2 bay leaves

3 pounds seafood (such as 1 pound shrimp, peeled and deveined; ½ pound crab meat, flaked; ½ pound sea scallops, quartered; 1 pound flaky white fish, such as snapper or cod)

1 loaf French bread, sliced and toasted

French-food lovers, fear not the long list of steps and ingredients for this traditional dish. It's easier than you think. Many of the ingredients are probably already in your pantry, and the rest can easily be found in your local grocery store. The key to great bouillabaisse is fresh seafood. We're talking fresh-from-the-sea fresh, not Joe's week-old specials. Nothing spoils a fish-based stew like subpar fish. Get to know the person at the fish counter and find out what's fresh that day. In fact, ask to sniff the fish before they wrap it up for you—you want it to smell like the sea. Much like paella, this dish has very flexible ingredients. It's part of the fun. Plus, you'll be amazed at how quickly and easily it comes together. It's time to start a French revolution—in your kitchen!

✳ ✳ ✳ ✳ ✳

1 Preheat the oven to 400°F.

2 In a heavy, ovenproof Dutch oven, melt the butter. Add the onion, bell pepper, and garlic, and sauté until they begin to soften, about 8 minutes. Add the tomato juice, tomato, flour, brown sugar, hot sauce, orange zest, curry powder, thyme, saffron, salt, and black pepper, and stir until well combined. Bring the mixture to a boil, stirring often. Reduce the heat to medium so the mixture is at a gentle simmer. Add the wine, lemon juice, ¼ cup parsley, and the bay leaves. Simmer, uncovered, for 10 to 15 minutes. Taste for seasoning. If you would like to brighten flavors, add a bit more lemon juice.

3 Add the seafood to the pan, stirring gently so as not to break up the fish. Place the pot in the oven and bake for

about 20 minutes or until the fish pieces are cooked through and flaky.

4 To serve, place two pieces of toasted bread in the bottom of eight large soup bowls. Ladle the bouillabaisse over the bread and garnish with the remaining 2 tablespoons parsley. Serve immediately.

Get to know Sriracha, one of Sandy's favorite sauces. Also known as "Rooster Sauce" for the rooster that emblazons the bottle's label, this Thai chili sauce is fantastically spicy. If you don't have any on hand, you can substitute Tabasco sauce. Careful, though—Tabasco sauce will have a more vinegary taste, so be sure to adjust the amount of lemon juice to about half.

When cooking for our business, Sandy is a stickler when it comes to proper *mise en place*. This is a French phrase meaning "everything in place," and it refers to having all your ingredients prepped, measured, and ready to go before you start cooking. With recipes that have many ingredients, such as this bouillabaisse, you will find that taking the time to do the prep first will actually save you time in the long run. When everything is laid out in front of you, you'll be more organized and efficient. (Plus, you will look like a real chef!)

Seafood Lasagna Rolls with Panko Crumb Topping

**MAKES 6 SERVINGS
(2 ROLLS PER PERSON)**

Panko Crumb Topping

1 cup panko bread crumbs

½ cup (1 stick) unsalted butter, melted

⅓ cup grated Parmesan cheese (1½ ounces)

2 tablespoons shallots, finely chopped

2 tablespoons chopped fresh flat-leaf parsley

½ teaspoon chopped fresh thyme leaves

Lasagna Rolls

Cooking spray

12 dried lasagna noodles

2 tablespoons unsalted butter

2 medium shallots, thinly sliced

1 red bell pepper, chopped

3 tablespoons all-purpose flour

2½ teaspoons salt

2 teaspoons ground white pepper

1 cup bottled clam juice

½ cup dry white wine

2 tablespoons sherry

Unlike layered lasagne, which can lose its shape and become messy when served, these individual rolls are an elegant alternative that look as lovely on the plate as they taste. Crisp white wine and the nutty flavors of sherry come together beautifully in a creamy white sauce, adding a delicate accent that's perfect for the shellfish. Easily portioned, this dish is excellent for entertaining. Remember to do your prep early, as this recipe does take some time to assemble.

1 To make the topping, put the bread crumbs, butter, Parmesan, shallots, parsley, and thyme in a medium bowl, and mix thoroughly. Set aside.

2 Preheat the oven to 375°F. Lightly coat a 9 x 13-inch casserole dish with cooking spray.

3 In a large pot of boiling salted water, cook the lasagna noodles according to the package instructions. Drain the noodles, rinse with cold water, and lay them flat on a baking sheet while you make the sauce.

4 In a small saucepan set over medium-high heat, melt the butter. Add the shallots and bell pepper, and sauté for about 3 minutes or until tender. Reduce the heat to medium and whisk in the flour, 1½ teaspoons of the salt, and 1 teaspoon of the white pepper. Cook for 2 minutes, whisking constantly, until the flour is cooked through. Pour in the clam juice, wine, and sherry and cook, whisking constantly, until a light sauce forms, 2 to 3 minutes. Add

the cream and cook, whisking frequently, until the sauce thickens, about 5 minutes. Remove the pan from heat. Add 1 cup of the cheese and the spinach, and cook until the spinach wilts. Set the sauce aside.

5   Rinse the seafood under cold running water. Drain thoroughly and pat dry with a paper towel to remove any excess liquid. In a large bowl, combine the shrimp, scallops, cod, and crab meat with the remaining 1 teaspoon salt and 1 teaspoon white pepper and the parsley. Add 1 cup of the sauce mixture and fold until well combined.

6   Spread a heaping ⅓ cup of the seafood mixture on each noodle, leaving a ½-inch border on the edges. Roll up each noodle.

7   Spread about ½ cup of the sauce on the bottom of the prepared casserole dish. Arrange the rolled lasagna noodles seam side down snugly in one layer over the sauce. Pour the remaining sauce over the rolls. Sprinkle the casserole with the remaining 1 cup cheese, and then top evenly with the crumb topping. Cover the dish with foil, and bake until the sauce is bubbling and the filling is just cooked through, about 30 minutes.

8   Preheat the broiler. Remove the foil from the dish, and broil casserole about 3 inches from the heat until the crumb topping is browned, 3 to 5 minutes. Let stand for 5 minutes before serving.

2 cups heavy cream

8 ounces Monterey jack cheese, grated (2 cups)

6 ounces fresh spinach leaves

1 pound shrimp, peeled and deveined

1 pound bay scallops

¾ pound cod, haddock, or other white fish fillets, cut into 1-inch cubes

½ pound lump crab meat

1 tablespoon chopped fresh flat-leaf parsley

Halibut Enchiladas with Salsa Verde

MAKES 5 SERVINGS

2 pounds halibut fillets

1 cup plus 2 tablespoons vegetable oil

Salt and freshly ground black pepper

1 tablespoon unsalted butter

½ cup chopped onion

¾ cup mayonnaise

¾ cup sour cream

1 (4-ounce) can diced green chiles

2 cups store-bought shredded Mexican cheese mix (8 ounces)

4 cups store-bought salsa verde, or homemade Salsa Verde (page 198)

10 8-inch corn tortillas

Upscale enchiladas? You betcha! Take your enchiladas to serious new heights by baking fresh halibut, instead of frying it, and cooking the enchiladas in a delicious tangy verde sauce. Serve with black beans sprinkled with Cotija cheese, and a simple side salad for a truly flavorful meal.

1 Preheat the oven to 350°F.

2 Lightly coat the halibut with 2 tablespoons of the vegetable oil and season it with salt and pepper. Put the halibut in a 9 x 13-inch casserole dish and bake for 25 minutes. Allow the halibut to cool, then flake it into a bowl. Keep the oven at 350°F.

3 Melt the butter in a sauté pan set over medium heat. Add the onion and cook until translucent, about 8 minutes. Transfer the onion to a medium bowl and add the mayonnaise, sour cream, chiles, and 1 cup of the cheese mix. Mix thoroughly.

4 Pour 2 cups of the verde sauce into the bottom of a 9 x 13-inch casserole dish. Set aside.

5 Heat the remaining 1 cup of vegetable oil in a sauté pan set over medium heat until just warm, then turn off the heat. Put one tortilla in the oil at a time and leave it in the oil for 5 seconds (you are looking to just make the tortilla pliable, not brown or crunchy). Transfer the tortilla to a cutting board. Put ¼ cup of the fish mixture on one end of the tortilla. Roll up the tortilla and put it on top of the sauce in the casserole dish, seam side down. Repeat until all ten

tortillas are filled, then pour the remaining 2 cups verde sauce over the top to coat the enchiladas entirely. Sprinkle the remaining 1 cup cheese mix over the top.

6 Bake for 25 minutes or until the sauce is bubbling slightly and the enchiladas are heated through.

Salsa verde is a versatile sauce that Sandy has in her refrigerator all the time. She likes to warm 1 cup of the sauce in the morning and pour it over eggs and toast for breakfast. It's a spicy way to start the day!

Shrimp with Seared Polenta

MAKES 6 SERVINGS

Seared Polenta

1 tablespoon unsalted butter

4 cups water

2 teaspoons salt

2¼ cups yellow cornmeal

¼ cup heavy cream

1 teaspoon dried thyme

Cooking spray

Shrimp

2 tablespoons olive oil

¼ pound pancetta, chopped

3 garlic cloves, minced

½ teaspoon red pepper flakes

1 (14-ounce) can diced tomatoes

1 pound large shrimp, peeled and deveined

¾ teaspoon salt

1 tablespoon chopped fresh flat-leaf parsley

Firm polenta serves as the base for a delectable shrimp sauce made with tomatoes, garlic, red pepper flakes, and crisp pancetta crumbles. Once seared, the polenta is perfectly crisp on the outside and velvety on the inside. You'll need to make the polenta a couple of hours before serving, since it needs time to cool and set before you can sear it. Luckily, it can be made ahead of time.

✳ ✳ ✳ ✳ ✳

1 For the seared polenta, lightly grease a 9 x 13-inch casserole dish with ½ tablespoon of the butter. Set aside.

2 Combine the water and salt in a medium saucepan and bring just to a boil. Whisk in the cornmeal and continue whisking until it starts to thicken, about 3 minutes. Stir in the cream and thyme. Reduce the heat to low and simmer, stirring constantly, until the polenta is very thick.

3 Pour the polenta into the prepared pan and brush the top with the remaining ½ tablespoon of the butter. Let it stand at room temperature until cool, then cover and refrigerate until chilled. (Polenta can be kept in the refrigerator for three days before using.)

4 When ready to use, turn the chilled polenta onto a cutting board, and cut into 12 triangles. Set aside.

5 For the shrimp, heat the olive oil in a sauté pan set over medium heat. Add the pancetta and cook until crisp, about 10 minutes. Remove the pancetta from the pan and set aside. Add the garlic and red pepper flakes to the pan and cook, stirring, until the garlic is pale golden, 2 to 3 minutes. Return the pancetta to the pan along with the tomatoes

and their juice. Bring to a simmer and cook until the liquid is reduced to about ¼ cup, 6 to 8 minutes. Add the shrimp and cook, stirring occasionally, until the shrimp are just cooked through, about 3 minutes. Season with the salt and garnish with the parsley.

6 Lightly grease a sauté pan with cooking spray. Sear the polenta triangles until all sides have a light golden crust, about 2 minutes per side. Place two triangles of polenta on each of six plates and top each with 1 cup of shrimp sauce.

Crystal loves the flavor of pancetta. If you are unable to find it at your local grocery, you can substitute with prosciutto or even bacon.

Savory Salmon Turnovers

MAKES 6 SERVINGS

½ cup long-grain white rice

2 tablespoons unsalted butter

1 leek, thinly sliced, white and pale green parts only

1 carrot, cut into thin strips

1 celery rib, cut into thin strips

1½ tablespoons all-purpose flour

1 teaspoon dried tarragon, crushed

Salt and freshly ground black pepper

1 cup whole milk

¼ cup heavy cream

2 tablespoons dry white wine

Cooking spray

3 sheets frozen puff pastry, thawed

6 (6-ounce each) salmon fillets, about 2½ inches thick, skin removed

1 egg

We actually got this brilliant idea from our World's Greatest Chicken Pot Pie recipe (page 48), borrowing some of its staple flavors to create an entirely new dish. The mild flavors of the tarragon and white wine sauce complement the leek mixture in this new creation. Baking the salmon *en croute* keeps the fish moist and seals in its natural flavors. When you find a flavor combination you love, experiment and find new ways to make it work for you!

✳ ✳ ✳ ✳ ✳

1 Cook the rice according to the package directions. Set aside.

2 Melt the butter in a heavy, medium skillet set over medium-low heat. Add the leek, carrot, and celery, and sauté until beginning to soften, about 4 minutes. Add the flour, tarragon, 1 teaspoon of salt, and 1 teaspoon of pepper, and cook for 1 minute. Add the milk and cream, and cook, stirring, until thickened and bubbly, about 8 minutes. Stir in the wine and heat thoroughly for an additional 2 minutes, stirring often. Remove from the heat and stir in the cooked rice. Set aside.

3 Preheat the oven to 400°F. Coat two 9 x 13-inch casserole dishes with cooking spray.

4 On a flat, lightly floured surface, roll the puff pastry sheets into 12-inch squares. Cut four equal squares from each sheet so that you have 12 squares total. Divide the rice mixture among six of the pastry squares, mounding the mixture into an oval shape with the ends toward two

corners of the pastry square. Set a salmon fillet on top of each rice oval and sprinkle with salt and pepper. Make an egg wash by lightly beating together the egg and 1 teaspoon water. Brush the edge of the puff pastry with the egg wash, then bring the pastry corners up around salmon (the pastry will not enclose the salmon completely.) Brush the edges of a second pastry square with egg wash and lay it on top of the salmon fillet, tucking its corners under the bottom of the pastry to enclose the fillet completely. Pinch the edges together to seal and brush the entire turnover with egg wash. Repeat for remaining turnovers. Cut a vent in the top of each turnover to allow steam to escape.

5 Arrange the salmon packages in the prepared casserole dishes, allowing each puff pastry package enough room to puff without touching each other. Bake until the pastry is golden brown and a thermometer inserted into the fish registers 145°F, about 30 minutes.

You can prepare this dish several hours ahead of time. Once you've made the turnovers, cover and chill them in the refrigerator until your guests arrive. Then, simply pop them in the preheated oven, serve, and enjoy. Easy entertaining at its best.

Lobster Boy *Casserole*

MAKES 4 TO 6 SERVINGS

7 tablespoons unsalted butter

1 medium shallot, thinly sliced

1 pound meat from cooked lobster tails (4 tails), cut into bite-size pieces (see tip)

3 tablespoons all-purpose flour

½ teaspoon dry mustard

Salt and freshly ground black pepper

2 cups light cream

3 tablespoons sherry

3 slices white bread, crusts removed and slices torn into small pieces

½ cup seasoned bread crumbs (see page 196)

Crystal's brother-in-law Jim is a native of Maine, and he has a passion so strong for lobster that we have nicknamed him "Lobster Boy." We have joked that if he were rich, he would eat lobster in some form or fashion every day—lobster rolls, lobster omelets, and even lobster casseroles. This casserole salutes you, Lobster Boy! We recommend serving it over buttered egg noodles that have been tossed with poppy seeds for color and a bit of a crunch.

1 Preheat the oven to 350°F.

2 Melt 4 tablespoons of the butter in a sauté pan set over medium heat. Add the shallot and cook for 3 minutes or until translucent. Add the lobster meat and cook for 2 minutes or until the lobster is heated through. In a separate bowl, combine the flour and dry mustard, and season with salt and pepper. Sprinkle the mixture over the lobster and toss to coat well. Add the cream slowly, stirring constantly, and cook until it thickens, about 6 minutes. Add the sherry and bread, and stir well.

3 Grease a 9 x 13-inch casserole dish with 1 tablespoon of the butter and pour in the lobster mixture. Melt the remaining 2 tablespoons of butter and stir in the bread crumbs, then sprinkle on top of the casserole.

4 Bake for 30 minutes or until the casserole is bubbly and browned on top.

If you don't want to be the one to do the deed, most fish markets will cook the lobster to your liking. All you'll need to do is take it home, remove the shells, grease your casserole dish, and get cooking!

Sherry versus cooking sherry: When cooking with high-quality ingredients such as fresh seafood, we recommend that you opt for the real thing! Cooking sherry is high in salt, and the quality just isn't good enough to stand up to the lovely buttery lobster in this dish.

Asparagus and Crab Casserole

MAKES 8 SERVINGS

2 tablespoons unsalted butter

2 tablespoons all-purpose flour

1⅔ cups whole milk

1 ounce Cheddar cheese, grated (¼ cup)

1 ounce Swiss cheese, grated (¼ cup)

1 teaspoon salt

⅛ teaspoon freshly ground black pepper

24 fresh asparagus spears

1 pound lump crab meat

1 cup grated Parmesan cheese (4 ounces)

Crystal *loves* crab. So much, in fact, that she is willing to risk physical harm to get it. You see, Crystal has recently developed an allergic reaction to crab meat. She feels as though the universe is playing some cruel joke on her—and she's just not ready to accept it. Allergy or not, this is one of her favorite casseroles. There is just something so irresistible about the sweetness of the crab and how it interacts with the earthy taste of the asparagus. Serve this creamy casserole over toasted French bread (much like an open-faced sandwich) and pour yourself a glass of a crisp white wine—you'll be very thankful that you are not allergic.

1 Preheat the oven to 375°F.

2 Melt the butter in a saucepan set over medium heat. Stir in the flour and cook, stirring, for 3 minutes. Gradually add the milk and stir until thick and smooth, about 5 minutes. Add the Cheddar and Swiss cheeses, and stir until melted. Add the salt and pepper. Set aside.

3 Hold an asparagus spear with both hands, about 2 inches from the ends. Gently bend the asparagus until it snaps. It will break at the point where the stem gets too tough to be enjoyable; discard the stem. Repeat for all your asparagus. Cook the asparagus in boiling water until just tender, 2 to 3 minutes. Drain.

4 Place the asparagus in a 9 x 13-inch casserole dish. Scatter the crab meat over the asparagus, then pour in the cheese sauce. Sprinkle with the Parmesan, then bake for about 30 minutes or until top is golden brown and the sauce is bubbling.

Crawfish Casserole

There is an old Louisiana legend that says that when the original Acadians fled Nova Scotia to head to Louisiana, the local lobsters followed them. During the long swim the lobsters lost a lot of weight and most of their length. By the time they reached the bayou swamps to reunite with the early Cajuns, they had turned into crawfish!

Crawfish, mudbugs, or crawdads—whatever you decide to call them, they're delicious. With Texas being so close to bayou country, we can't help but love these cute crustaceans. Though resembling tiny lobsters, only the extremely tasty tail is edible. When they are cooked with spicy Cajun flavors, you have yourself a mighty fine treat. Just remember that Louisiana crawfish are seasonal. A consistent supply can't be counted on except between early March and mid-June, with the height of the season mid-March to mid-May. If crawfish are not available, peeled and deveined shrimp serve as a good substitute.

✳ ✳ ✳ ✳ ✳

1 Preheat the oven to 300°F. Lightly coat a 9 x 13-inch casserole dish with cooking spray.

2 Melt the butter in a large sauté pan set over medium heat. Add the onion and cook for about 8 minutes. Add the crawfish, bell pepper, and green onions, and cook for 5 minutes. Add the mushrooms, parsley, garlic powder, cayenne, black pepper, and salt and cook for 5 minutes. Remove the pan from heat, add 2 cups of the bread crumbs and the egg, and stir well.

3 Pour the mixture into the casserole dish and top with the remaining ½ cup bread crumbs. Bake for 25 minutes or until the casserole is set and the bread crumbs are golden brown.

MAKES 6 SERVINGS

Cooking spray

½ cup (1 stick) unsalted butter

1 cup chopped onion

2 pounds meat from crawfish tails (about 14 pounds whole crawfish)

½ cup chopped green bell pepper

½ cup chopped green onions, green parts only

1 (10-ounce) container sliced white button mushrooms

¼ cup chopped fresh flat-leaf parsley

1 teaspoon garlic powder

½ teaspoon cayenne

½ teaspoon freshly ground black pepper

½ teaspoon salt

2½ cups seasoned bread crumbs (see page 196)

1 egg, beaten

Meet the Lighter Side of The Casserole Queens

Cutting calories doesn't mean you have to cut flavor. The Casserole Queens are all about comfort food and the satisfaction of a good meal. So, do you really think we'd include recipes that didn't please the palate? You can rest assured that even though we've altered these recipes, you won't leave the dinner table feeling unsatisfied. Our approach about healthy eating is about neither sacrifice nor denial; instead, it is about taste and enjoyment, moderation, variety, and balance. By using the right combinations of fresh ingredients, seasonings, and herbs, lower fat cheeses, and heart-healthy fats, we trimmed calories without sacrificing that fabulous flavor you expect from a comfort-food dish. Who says watching your diet has to be boring? Not the Queens!

Mamma Mia! Lasagne

Beef and Rice Fiesta Bake

Beef-Stuffed Cabbage Rolls

"I'll Never Go Hungary Again" Goulash

Mandarin Meatloaf

Damn Skinny Yankee Pot Roast

Not Your Average Tamale Pie

Queen Ranch Casserole

Chicken Tetrazzini

Tuscan Ziti Bake

Summer Halibut with Dill

Mediterranean Medley

Baked Fish and Vegetables with Tangy Caper Sauce

Red Snapper Veracruz

Black Bean Enchilada Casserole

Mamma Mia! Lasagne

MAKES 10 SERVINGS

1 pound lean ground beef round

Salt

½ teaspoon freshly ground black pepper, plus more to taste

Cooking spray

1 cup chopped onion

5 garlic cloves, minced

1 (28-ounce) can diced tomatoes

1 (14½-ounce) can Italian-style stewed tomatoes

1 (8-ounce) can tomato sauce

1 (6-ounce) can tomato paste

¼ cup dried parsley

2 teaspoons dried oregano

1 teaspoon dried basil

2 cups nonfat cottage cheese

½ cup finely grated Parmesan cheese (2 ounces)

1 (15-ounce) container nonfat ricotta

1 egg white

12 no-boil lasagna noodles

8 ounces store-bought shredded Italian cheese mix (2 cups)

Just like mamma used to make, only better for you! By using a mixture of fat-free ricotta and low-fat cottage cheese, we've slashed loads of unnecessary calories while maintaining a true traditional taste. People all over Austin have fallen in love with our layers of lasagna noodles combined with our homemade meat sauce and light cheeses. It tastes so much like the real deal that you won't believe it's light.

✳ ✳ ✳ ✳ ✳

1 Season the meat with salt and pepper, and put it in a large saucepan set over medium heat. Cook the meat, breaking up any lumps with the back of a spoon, until browned throughout, about 10 minutes. Drain the fat from the meat and set the meat aside.

2 Wipe out the pan with a paper towel. Coat the pan with cooking spray and set it over medium heat. Add the onion and garlic, and sauté for 8 minutes. Return the meat to the pan. Add the diced tomatoes, stewed tomatoes, tomato sauce, tomato paste, 2 tablespoons of the parsley, the oregano, and basil. Stir well and bring the mixture to a boil. Cover the pan, reduce the heat to low, and simmer for 15 minutes. Uncover the pan and simmer for 20 more minutes. Remove the pan from heat.

3 Preheat the oven to 350°F. Coat a 9 x 13-inch casserole dish with cooking spray.

4 Combine the remaining 2 tablespoons of parsley, the cottage cheese, Parmesan cheese, ricotta, and egg white in a large bowl. Stir well, and set aside.

5 Spread ¾ cup of the tomato mixture in the bottom of the prepared casserole dish. Arrange four of the lasagna noodles over the tomato mixture; top with half of the cottage cheese mixture, 2¼ cups of the tomato mixture, and ⅔ cup of the Italian cheese mix. Repeat the layers once, then end with an additional layer of noodles. Spread the remaining tomato mixture over the top.

6 Cover with foil and bake for 1 hour. Uncover the dish, sprinkle the lasagna with the remaining ⅓ cup of cheese mix, and bake for 10 more minutes. Let the lasagne stand for 10 minutes before serving.

Great for freezing! See our Freezer Tips on pages 23–27.

This dish has plenty of sauce and is perfect for using no-boil lasagna noodles, which will save you the hassle of first cooking dried lasagna noodles.

Beef and Rice *Fiesta Bake*

MAKES 6 TO 8 SERVINGS

Cooking spray

½ pound lean ground beef

Salt and freshly ground black pepper

1 cup chopped onion

1 cup chopped green bell pepper

½ cup water

2 (14½-ounce) cans diced tomatoes

2 (4½-ounce) cans chopped green chiles

2 tablespoons chili powder

2 teaspoons ground cumin

1½ teaspoons sugar

1 teaspoon dried oregano

4 cups cooked long-grain rice (see page 195)

1 cup fat-free sour cream

½ cup sliced green onions, green parts only

½ cup skim milk

3 ounces reduced-fat sharp Cheddar cheese, grated (¾ cup)

Say no to grapefruit diets, and yes to feeling satisfied. Similar to a burrito filling, this casserole boasts a creamy rice mixture made with low-fat sour cream and green onions, all covered in a spicy meat sauce and topped with reduced-fat Cheddar. Round out a healthy dinner by serving this dish with either a fruit or green salad and dinner rolls. It's also perfect to use as a filling for whole wheat or corn tortillas.

1 Preheat the oven to 375°F. Coat a 9 x 13-inch casserole dish with cooking spray.

2 Season the beef with salt and pepper. Put the beef, onion, and bell pepper into a large skillet set over medium-high heat. Cook, breaking up any lumps with the back of a spoon, until the meat is browned, about 8 minutes. Add the water, diced tomatoes, green chiles, chili powder, cumin, sugar, and oregano. Stir and bring the mixture to a boil. Cover the skillet, reduce the heat to low, and simmer for 10 minutes. Uncover the skillet and simmer the mixture for 2 more minutes. Remove the skillet from the heat, and set aside.

3 Combine the rice, sour cream, green onions, and milk in a bowl. Spoon the rice mixture into the prepared casserole dish. Top with the beef mixture and sprinkle the top with the cheese. Bake for 30 minutes or until heated through and the cheese on top is bubbling.

Great for freezing! See our Freezer Tips on pages 23–27.

Beef-Stuffed Cabbage Rolls

Or as we like to call them—Hungarian pigs in a blanket! (We're a bit silly, if you haven't noticed.) This dish traveled into our hearts long ago and has satisfied our families for generations. It was surprising to us that this comfort food that we grew up on wasn't that bad for you! Made with lean ground beef, rice, and veggies, and covered in a tomato sauce, these rolls will fill you up but not weigh you down.

MAKES 8 TO 10 SERVINGS

1 large head of green cabbage

1 pound lean ground beef chuck

⅓ cup cooked long-grain white rice (see page 195)

1 small onion, grated

2 large eggs

2 teaspoons salt

½ teaspoon freshly ground black pepper

1 large onion, sliced

3 (14½-ounce) cans diced tomatoes

1 (15-ounce) can tomato sauce

4 teaspoons fresh lemon juice (from 1 large lemon)

¼ cup packed light brown sugar

1 Preheat the oven to 350°F.

2 Remove 15 large leaves from the cabbage and trim off the thickest part of each leaf. Pour boiling water over the cabbage and let the leaves soak until they are pliable, about 4 minutes. Remove from the water, pat dry, and set aside.

3 In a large bowl, combine the beef, rice, grated onion, eggs, 1 teaspoon of the salt, and ¼ teaspoon of the black pepper. Place ¼ cup of the meat mixture in the cupped part of each of the softened cabbage leaves. Fold over the sides of each leaf and roll them up. Recipe will make 8 to 10 rolls. Place the remaining 5 cabbage leaves in the bottom of a 9 x 13-inch casserole dish. Arrange layers of cabbage rolls seam side down, then add a layer of sliced onion over the cabbage rolls. Top the onion slices with another layer of cabbage rolls.

4 In a large bowl, combine the tomatoes, tomato sauce, lemon juice, remaining 1 teaspoon salt, and remaining ¼ teaspoon pepper. Pour over the cabbage rolls. Bake until bubbling, about 30 minutes. Sprinkle the casserole with the brown sugar, cover the dish with foil, and continue baking for 1 hour. Remove and serve hot. Spoon pan juices over rolls.

"I'll Never Go Hungary Again" Goulash

MAKES 8 TO 10 SERVINGS

Cooking spray

2 cups thinly sliced onions

1 cup thinly sliced celery

2 garlic cloves, minced

1½ pounds lean ground beef

1 (6-ounce) can tomato paste

3 tablespoons all-purpose flour

1 tablespoon paprika

4 cups water

2 (14½-ounce) cans stewed tomatoes

1½ pounds Yukon Gold potatoes, peeled and cut into ½-inch cubes

1 tablespoon low-sodium beef bouillon granules

2 teaspoons salt

1 teaspoon ground marjoram

⅛ teaspoon freshly ground black pepper

1 bay leaf

Pinch of parsley flakes

This Hungarian-style dish reminds us of learning to cook on our own while in college. The term "goulash" is very loose in its definition as it was a dish invented for using leftovers—or in our case, whatever we could find in the kitchen!

Sandy, in particular, has fond memories of goulash. She was the last of the four Pollock sisters to leave home. Lucky for Sandy, her sister Yvette lived nearby. While Sandy was living with her parents and attending college, Yvette was a young schoolteacher, just getting started in her career. Yvette didn't have a lot of money, but she was always generous and creative. From time to time, she would invite Sandy and her parents over for goulash, asking, "Oh, would you mind bringing over a can of corn from the house? And could you grab some cheese? And some beef? Oh, and an onion?" It turned out that her goulash was composed of whatever the Pollocks had in their fridge or pantry at the time. But Yvette would always set the table for the family and turn the borrowed ingredients into the most delicious meal.

1 Preheat the oven to 325°F.

2 Coat a 4-quart oven-safe saucepan or Dutch oven with cooking spray and set over medium heat. Add the onions and celery, and sauté for 8 minutes. Add the garlic and sauté for 5 more minutes or until the onions are translucent. Add the beef, tomato paste, flour, and paprika; cook for 5 minutes, stirring constantly. Stir in the water, tomatoes, potatoes, bouillon, salt, marjoram, pepper, bay leaf, and parsley. Bring to a boil, then remove the pot from the heat and cover. Place the pan in the oven and cook for 1½ hours or until bubbling and potatoes can easily be pierced with a knife. Stir every ½ hour.

Mandarin Meatloaf

Fruit in a meatloaf? What were we thinking? Trust us; we thought the exact same thing when Crystal's sister, Cindy, suggested it one night in our test kitchen. But since Cindy is usually right (don't even bother trying to play a game of Trivial Pursuit with her), we gave it a whirl and it worked! In fact, the sweetness from the mandarin orange brings an exciting new twist to this old-time dish. As soon as you try it, you'll understand. Substituting ground turkey keeps the calories and fat in check, and when served with a side of stir-fried veggies and brown rice, this healthy meal is sure to become a regular household favorite.

MAKES 6 SERVINGS

Cooking spray

1 pound ground turkey breast

½ pound lean ground pork

1 cup chopped green onions, green parts only

1 cup panko bread crumbs

½ cup chopped red bell pepper

½ cup chopped mandarin orange (drained, if using canned)

½ cup canned water chestnuts, chopped and drained

½ cup hoisin sauce

3 garlic cloves, minced

2 large egg whites

1 tablespoon low-sodium soy sauce

1 tablespoon grated fresh ginger

¼ teaspoon salt

1 Preheat the oven to 350°F. Coat a 9 x 5-inch loaf pan with cooking spray.

2 Combine the turkey, pork, green onions, panko bread crumbs, bell pepper, orange, water chestnuts, ¼ cup of the hoisin sauce, the garlic, egg whites, soy sauce, ginger, and salt in a large bowl.

3 Put the mixture into the prepared loaf pan and spread the remaining ¼ cup hoisin sauce over the top of the meatloaf. Bake for 1 hour 15 minutes or until a meat thermometer registers 180°F. Let it stand for 5 minutes before serving.

Use a small funnel to quickly and easily separate an egg. The white will go through, while the yolk will stay in the top of the funnel.

Damn Skinny Yankee Pot Roast

MAKES 10 SERVINGS

2 teaspoons olive oil

1 (4-pound) boneless beef chuck roast, trimmed

1 tablespoon kosher salt

1 tablespoon freshly ground black pepper

4 garlic cloves, minced

3 cups low-sodium beef broth (page 201)

1 (6-ounce) can tomato paste

2 teaspoons sugar

2 tablespoons Worcestershire sauce

1¼ pounds small red potatoes

1 pound carrots, peeled and cut into 1-inch pieces

6 celery ribs, cut into 3-inch pieces

2 medium onions, quartered

2 tablespoons fresh lemon juice

2 tablespoons chopped fresh flat-leaf parsley

We all have a friend who can literally eat whatever she wants and continue to stay in shape. One of Crystal's dear friends, Carolyn, is that type of person: a Yankee from New Jersey—and a skinny one at that. Lucky for her, she introduced Crystal to this pot roast, and their friendship took off. Crystal soon found out that Carolyn actually cooks everything with lighter ingredients. Now we're on to Carolyn's secret!

1 Preheat the oven to 300°F.

2 Heat the olive oil in a large Dutch oven set over medium-high heat. Season the roast with salt and pepper. Put the roast in the pan and brown it on all sides, about 4 minutes per side. Add the garlic to the pan, and sauté until lightly browned, about 1 minute. Return the roast to the pan. In a separate bowl, combine the broth, tomato paste, sugar, and Worcestershire sauce and stir until the sugar dissolves. Pour over the roast and bring to a simmer.

3 Cover the Dutch oven, transfer to the oven, and roast for 2 hours. Add the potatoes, carrots, celery, and onions, in that order, to the pot. Cover and roast for 1 more hour, or until the vegetables are tender and the meat has an internal temperature of 140°F (medium rare). Remove the roast from the pan and set it on a cutting board to rest for 20 minutes. Strain the vegetables out of the liquid in the pan. Pour this liquid into a medium saucepan, set over medium-high heat, and reduce by half. Stir in the lemon juice.

4 Slice the roast. Place two slices of meat on each plate. Ladle sauce over the meat and garnish with the parsley.

Not Your Average Tamale Pie

Tamales are a *huge* part of the Christmas celebration and tradition in the Rio Grande Valley, where Sandy was born and raised. As such, the holiday season simply wouldn't be complete without eating copious amounts of tamales.

Tamales are fun to make, but very time-consuming, so many people simply purchase them from a local restaurant. We go to Delia's in Edinburg, Texas. Around Christmastime, they make about 25,000 tamales and become so busy that the doors are closed to regular customers and the police are dispatched to direct traffic. If your order isn't in at least two weeks prior to Christmas, then you're out of luck! Our spin on the tamale is a casserole that saves you both calories and countless hours of preparation.

✳ ✳ ✳ ✳ ✳

1 Preheat the oven to 400°F. Coat a 9 x 13-inch casserole dish with cooking spray.

2 Coat a large sauté pan with cooking spray and set it over medium-high heat. Add the turkey, onion, and poblano pepper and season with salt and pepper. Cook until the meat is browned throughout, about 7 minutes; drain well. Return the mixture to the pan and add the corn, tomatoes, cumin, chili powder, and garlic powder. Bring the mixture to a simmer and cook for 10 minutes. Pour the mixture into the prepared casserole dish.

3 Prepare the cornbread mix according to the package instructions. Pour the mixture over the top of the casserole. Bake for 20 to 25 minutes or until the topping is cooked and golden brown.

MAKES 6 TO 8 SERVINGS

Cooking spray

1 pound lean ground turkey

1 medium onion, chopped

1 poblano pepper, roasted, seeded, and chopped

Salt and freshly ground black pepper

1 (15¼-ounce) can whole kernel corn, drained

1 (14-ounce) can diced tomatoes, drained

1½ tablespoons ground cumin

1 tablespoon chili powder

¼ teaspoon garlic powder

1 (8½-ounce) package cornbread mix, such as Jiffy muffin mix

Queen Ranch *Casserole*

MAKES 6 SERVINGS

3 large whole boneless, skinless chicken breasts

1 tablespoon olive oil

Salt and freshly ground black pepper

1 tablespoon unsalted butter

1 medium onion, chopped

1 (14-ounce) can chicken broth, or 2 cups homemade chicken broth (page 200)

4 teaspoons cornstarch

1 (10-ounce) can Rotel tomatoes or diced tomatoes with green chiles

1 (8-ounce) can diced green chiles

6 corn tortillas, cut into bite-size pieces

4 ounces light Velveeta cheese, cut into ½-inch cubes (1 cup)

Garlic salt

All hail to the Queen! If you're a fan of our Traditional King Ranch Casserole (page 41), you will love this lighter version, which delivers on taste but not on fat. We cut out the creamy soups to home in on the flavors from the green chiles and Rotel tomatoes. That's not to say that this dish is super-spicy; it has a kick, but is overall very fresh.

The cornstarch and broth mixture is called a slurry, and is used to thicken soups, stews, and sauces. Here are a few tips for making a slurry: Never add cornstarch directly to a hot liquid or it will lump; slurries should be 1 part cornstarch to 2 parts liquid, and, when stirred, should have the consistency of heavy cream; if you don't have cornstarch, you can substitute flour—just use twice as much.

1 Preheat the oven to 350°F.

2 Coat the chicken breasts with the olive oil, then season with salt and pepper. Put the chicken on a baking sheet. Bake for 15 to 20 minutes or until no longer pink. Remove the pan from the oven and let the chicken cool. When it is cool enough to handle, dice it and set aside.

3 Melt the butter in a medium saucepan set over medium heat. Add the onion and cook until translucent, about 8 minutes. Add the cooked chicken. In a small bowl, whisk together the broth and cornstarch until smooth. Add the cornstarch mixture to the chicken mixture and cook for 5 minutes. Add the tomatoes and chiles and cook until thickened, about 6 minutes.

4 In the bottom of a 9 x 13-inch casserole dish, layer the tortilla pieces, cheese cubes, and chicken mixture, sprinkling each layer with garlic salt to taste. Bake for 30 minutes or until the cheese is melted and bubbling around the edges.

Great for freezing! See our Freezer Tips on pages 23–27.

The Queens are far from being food snobs. Heck, we love us some Velveeta cheese! We can't help it; it's in our blood. Don't believe us? Well, here's proof: When growing up, Sandy's mom worked as the postmaster for the post office in Hargill, Texas. (She just recently retired after forty-four years of service!) Her office was two blocks from their house. Every single day at 12:04 p.m., she would run in the door of home and demand that the TV be turned to whatever channel the soap opera *All My Children* was on. She then proceeded to prepare her lunch, which was a sandwich made with brown bread, mayo, sliced raw onion, and lots of Velveeta cheese. She ate this every single day. (Seriously!)

Chicken *Tetrazzini*

MAKES 6 TO 8 SERVINGS

Cooking spray

½ (16-ounce) box spaghetti

3 whole boneless, skinless chicken breasts

1 tablespoon olive oil

Salt and freshly ground black pepper

1 tablespoon unsalted butter

1 cup finely chopped onion

1 cup finely chopped celery

1 (8-ounce) container sliced button mushrooms

¾ teaspoon salt

½ cup dry sherry

½ cup all-purpose flour

1 (10¾-ounce) can low-sodium chicken broth

1 (4-ounce) package low-fat cream cheese

1⅓ cups grated Parmesan cheese (5½ ounces)

½ cup panko bread crumbs

Contrary to popular belief, chicken tetrazzini was served at many upscale restaurants throughout the United States in the early 1900s. The dish was inspired and named after the great Italian opera star Luisa Tetrazzini, and it was widely popular. In fact, it was so popular that home cooks everywhere began trying to re-create the famous dish in their homes, and it lost its appeal as a gourmet delicacy in fine dining establishments. Lucky for us at home, we can still enjoy this amazingly good comfort dish with our family and friends, unfettered by any unnecessary pretenses.

Typically it is made with heavy creams and lots of butter, but we have found some healthier substitutions, such as low-fat cream cheese, which still provides the decadence and creaminess of the original. The opera isn't over until the fat lady sings, but this much lighter version of a comfort food favorite will leave you enjoying the music!

✳   ✳   ✳   ✳   ✳

1 Preheat the oven to 350°F. Lightly coat a 9 x 13-inch casserole dish with cooking spray.

2 Bring a large pot of heavily salted water to a boil. Break the noodles in half and cook according to package instructions. Drain the pasta and set aside.

3 Coat the chicken pieces with olive oil and season with salt and pepper. Place the chicken on a baking sheet and bake for 15 to 20 minutes or until no longer pink. Remove the baking sheet from the oven and let the chicken cool. When cool enough to handle, dice it and set aside.

4 In same pot as you cooked the noodles in, melt the butter over medium heat. Add the onion, celery, and mushrooms, and cook, stirring, until soft, about 8 minutes. Season with the salt, add the sherry, and cook for about 1 minute.

Gradually add the flour to the pot while stirring to coat the vegetables. Cook, stirring constantly, until the mixture is thick, about 5 minutes. Begin gradually adding the chicken broth while stirring constantly. Bring the mixture to a boil, then reduce the heat to low. Simmer for about 5 minutes or until thickened. Add the cream cheese and stir until melted. Add 1 cup of the Parmesan cheese to the pasta and cooked chicken and stir until combined. Pour the mixture into the prepared casserole dish.

5 Mix the bread crumbs with the remaining 1/3 cup of Parmesan cheese in a small mixing bowl. Sprinkle the topping evenly over the casserole. Bake for 30 minutes or until bubbly and browned on top. Let the casserole rest for 10 minutes before serving.

Tuscan Ziti Bake

MAKES 6 SERVINGS

Cooking spray

½ (16-ounce) box dried ziti

8 ounces hot Italian turkey sausage, casings removed

1½ teaspoons olive oil

5 cups thinly sliced zucchini (about 1½ pounds)

2 cups sliced onions (2 large onions)

3 garlic cloves, minced

½ teaspoon salt

¼ teaspoon freshly ground black pepper

¼ teaspoon red pepper flakes

½ cup fat-free, low-sodium chicken broth

¼ cup dry white wine

1 tablespoon all-purpose flour

2 ounces feta cheese, crumbled (½ cup)

2 ounces part-skim mozzarella cheese, shredded (½ cup)

As well as being inexpensive and easy to make, pasta is actually low in fat. It typically tends to be what we combine it with (and how much we consume) that gets us into trouble! But if you are still worried about carbohydrates, you can always opt for low-carb or whole wheat pasta. Instead of substituting the pasta, we avoided calorie pitfalls by adding lots of zucchini and using naturally lower fat cheeses, such as feta. The addition of hot Italian turkey sausage and red pepper flakes adds just the right amount of heat to keep your taste buds happy. Pair this dish with your favorite salad to make a quick and satisfying meal any night of the week.

1 Preheat the oven to 350°F. Coat a 9 x 13-inch baking dish with cooking spray.

2 Cook the pasta in boiling salted water for 6 minutes. Drain well and set aside.

3 Coat a large skillet with cooking spray and set it over medium-high heat. Add the sausage to the pan and cook, breaking up any lumps with the back of a spoon, until thoroughly browned, about 8 minutes. Transfer the sausage to a plate and set aside.

4 Wipe out the pan with a paper towel, set over medium-high heat, and add the olive oil. Add the zucchini, onions, garlic, salt, pepper, and red pepper flakes. Cook, stirring occasionally, for 10 minutes or until the vegetables are tender and the zucchini begins to brown.

5 In a small bowl, whisk together the broth, wine, and flour. Add the broth mixture to the pan with the vegetables and cook for 2 minutes. Combine the vegetable mixture, pasta, sausage, and feta cheese in a large bowl; toss well. Spoon the pasta mixture into the prepared baking dish. Sprinkle the mozzarella cheese evenly over the top. Bake for 20 minutes or until bubbly and lightly browned.

Great for freezing! See our Freezer Tips on pages 23–27.

For quickly slicing zucchini, we love using our hand-held mandoline. Just be extra careful not to move too fast—that blade is sharp!

Summer Halibut *with Dill*

MAKES 4 TO 6 SERVINGS

1 tablespoon extra-virgin olive oil, plus more to drizzle

4 (6-ounce each) halibut fillets

Salt and freshly ground black pepper

3 tablespoons chopped fresh dill

2 ripe but firm medium tomatoes, seeded and sliced

½ cup red onion, thinly sliced

½ cup seasoned bread crumbs (see page 196)

½ cup grated Parmesan cheese (2 ounces)

Dill is one of our favorite summertime herbs. Its fresh, clean flavor is perfect for a flaky white fish like halibut. It's lovely served with wild brown rice and crisp green beans. You can also make this with haddock or red snapper.

1 Preheat the oven to 450°F.

2 Lightly coat a 9 x 13-inch casserole dish with olive oil. Place the fish fillets in the dish, overlapping them slightly if necessary, and season with salt and pepper. Sprinkle half of the dill over the fish and cover with the sliced tomatoes. Scatter the onion slices over the top and sprinkle with the remaining dill. Drizzle with the olive oil and season lightly with salt and pepper. Sprinkle the seasoned bread crumbs and Parmesan cheese over the top.

3 Bake for 25 to 30 minutes or until bubbling on the sides and the fish is cooked through. Serve hot.

Mediterranean Medley

Light on calories. More than delicious. We took the best of Mediterranean flavors and brought them together harmoniously in this fresh and delightful dish. Scrumptious shrimp and feta are baked with fresh herbs and tomatoes in a light sauce of wine and clam juice that is perfect for serving over a bed of linguini.

✳   ✳   ✳   ✳   ✳

1 Preheat the oven to 450°F. Coat a 9 x 13-inch casserole dish with cooking spray.

2 Rinse the shrimp and pat dry with paper towels. Combine the shrimp and lemon juice in a large bowl and toss well. Set aside.

3 Coat a large skillet with cooking spray and set over medium-high heat. Put the onion in the pan and cook for 8 minutes or until translucent. Add the garlic and cook for 1 minute. Add the tomatoes, clam juice, wine, oregano, basil, 1 tablespoon parsley, and pepper. Bring the mixture to a boil, reduce the heat, and simmer for 5 minutes. Remove the pan from heat. Stir in the reserved shrimp.

4 Put the shrimp mixture in the prepared casserole dish. Sprinkle the feta cheese evenly over the top. Bake for 12 minutes or until the shrimp are opaque and the cheese is melted. Remove the dish from the oven and sprinkle the remaining 1 tablespoon parsley over the top. Serve immediately over the linguini, with lemon wedges on the side.

MAKES 4 SERVINGS

Cooking spray

1½ pounds large shrimp, peeled and deveined

1 tablespoon fresh lemon juice

½ cup chopped onion

2 garlic cloves, minced

3 plum tomatoes, diced

3 tablespoons bottled clam juice

3 tablespoons dry white wine

2 teaspoons chopped fresh oregano

1 tablespoon chopped fresh basil

2 tablespoons chopped fresh flat-leaf parsley

¼ teaspoon freshly ground black pepper

3 ounces feta cheese, crumbled (¾ cup)

1 (16-ounce) box linguine, cooked

4 lemon wedges, for garnish

Baked Fish and Vegetables with Tangy Caper Sauce

MAKES 6 SERVINGS

2 pounds red potatoes, peeled and cut into ⅛-inch slices (about 6 cups)

4 cups thinly sliced fennel (about 2 small bulbs)

1 tablespoon olive oil

¾ teaspoon salt

½ teaspoon freshly ground black pepper

1 teaspoon fennel seeds

3 garlic cloves, minced

1 (28-ounce) can whole tomatoes, drained and chopped

¾ cup dry white wine

6 tablespoons chopped fresh flat-leaf parsley

2 tablespoons grated lemon zest

3 teaspoons chopped fresh oregano

6 (6-ounce each) sea bass fillets, or other firm white fish fillets

Tangy Caper Sauce (recipe follows)

"Good for you" doesn't have to mean "bland." Crystal is a sucker for lots of flavor, and this dish is an extravaganza for her palate! It's light, fresh, and oh-so-flavorful. While the fish and roasted vegetables have a wonderful taste all on their own, Crystal adores the tangy caper sauce that makes this dish sing! Capers—small green pockets of salty goodness—are actually the unopened flower buds of a Mediterranean bush, *Capparis spinosa*. Once harvested, they are dried in the sun and then pickled in either a vinegar brine or packed in salt. There is a rather large variety of capers, varying in size and origin. Feel free to experiment to find the ones you like best, but we typically prefer the smaller nonpareille size that hails from southern France. If you are trying to watch the amount of salt in your diet, rinse the capers and pat dry with a towel before adding them to the sauce.

1 Preheat the oven to 450°F.

2 Combine the potatoes, fennel, 2 teaspoons of the oil, ¼ teaspoon of the salt, and ¼ teaspoon of the pepper in a 9 x 13-inch casserole dish; toss gently to coat. Bake the vegetables for 30 minutes or until they can easily be pierced with a fork.

3 Heat the remaining 1 teaspoon of oil in a medium skillet. Add the fennel seeds and garlic, and sauté for 1 minute. Add ¼ teaspoon of the salt, ⅛ teaspoon of the pepper, the tomatoes, wine, 4 tablespoons of the parsley, 1 tablespoon of the lemon zest, and the oregano to the pan. Bring the mixture to a boil, reduce the heat to low, and simmer for 8 minutes.

4 Sprinkle the fish fillets with the remaining ¼ teaspoon salt and the remaining ⅛ teaspoon pepper. Arrange the fillets over the potato mixture in the casserole dish. Sprinkle with the remaining tablespoon of lemon zest and spread the tomato mixture over the fish. Bake at 450°F for 20 minutes or until the fish flakes easily with a fork. Sprinkle with the remaining 2 tablespoons parsley. Spoon the caper sauce over the fish before serving.

Tangy Caper Sauce

MAKES ¼ CUP SAUCE

2 tablespoons fresh lemon juice

2 tablespoons extra-virgin olive oil

1½ teaspoons chopped fresh oregano

1 teaspoon salt

1 teaspoon grated lemon zest

2 garlic cloves, minced

3 tablespoons capers, drained

Dash of freshly ground black pepper

Put the lemon juice, olive oil, oregano, salt, lemon zest, garlic, capers, and pepper in a small bowl. Whisk to combine.

Red Snapper Veracruz

MAKES 8 SERVINGS

4 tablespoons (½ stick) unsalted butter

1 medium onion, chopped

1 (8-ounce) container sliced button mushrooms

½ green bell pepper, chopped

1 fresh jalapeño pepper, chopped (half the seeds removed for less heat)

1 (14¾-ounce) can tomato puree

1 (14¾-ounce) can diced tomatoes, drained

½ cup dry white wine

4 tablespoons chili sauce (such as Heinz)

3 tablespoons fresh lemon juice

3 tablespoons capers, drained

1 tablespoon chopped fresh flat-leaf parsley

2 garlic cloves, minced

½ tablespoon dried thyme

¼ teaspoon salt, plus more to taste

2 pounds fresh red snapper fillets

½ pound shrimp, peeled and deveined

Freshly ground black pepper

Sometimes we forget that there is more to Mexican food than our favorite enchiladas and puffy tacos. In fact, there are many specialty seafood dishes throughout the country, varying in style and preparation, yet equally delicious. Veracruz is a central Mexican city on the Gulf of Mexico, and it's where many Spanish conquistadors landed when first coming to the Americas. Here, culinary traditions began to meld—not only Spanish but also Mediterranean, French, and Caribbean. The result is *Veracruzano*—Veracruz style. We love serving our version of this dish over a bed of fluffy quinoa, which is an excellent vehicle for soaking up the delicious juices.

1 Preheat the oven to 425°F.

2 In a large sauté pan set over medium-high heat, melt the butter. Add the onion, mushrooms, bell pepper, and jalapeño, and cook until softened, about 8 minutes. Add the tomato puree, diced tomatoes, wine, chili sauce, lemon juice, capers, parsley, garlic, thyme, and salt, and cook for 5 minutes.

3 Pour half of the sauce into the bottom of a 9 x 13-inch casserole dish. Season the snapper fillets and the shrimp with salt and pepper, and lay them on top of the sauce. Pour the remaining sauce over the seafood. Bake for 15 to 18 minutes or until the fish is flaky.

Never heard of quinoa? Crystal invites you to get to know one of her favorite ingredients. Although quinoa (pronounced keen-wah) has been around for centuries, it isn't a mainstream pantry item in American kitchens. It has a similar texture to that of couscous or rice, with a slight crunch and a somewhat nutty flavor when cooked. Quinoa is considered a super food because it contains more protein than any other grain, and this protein is complete, containing all nine essential amino acids. Look for quinoa at your local grocery. Your body will thank you for it.

Black Bean Enchilada Casserole

MAKES 6 TO 8 SERVINGS

Cooking spay

10 6-inch corn tortillas

2 (14½-ounce) can diced tomatoes

1½ cups chopped green onions, green parts only

1 cup chopped onion

1 cup store-bought salsa or Salsa Rio Grande (page 197)

1 teaspoon ground cumin

2 (11-ounce) cans black bean soup

1 (15-ounce) can black beans, rinsed and drained

10 ounces reduced-fat Cheddar cheese, shredded (2½ cups)

Enjoy this flavorful Mexican dish with a casserole twist that's not only easy to put together but adds pure spice to the dinner routine. Since this recipe calls for you to layer ingredients as a stack, versus individually hand-rolling the enchiladas, we recommend that you bake the corn tortillas separately in the oven until crisp. With traditional enchiladas, the corn tortillas become mushy, but by toasting them in the oven, they help this casserole keep its shape. Serve with light sour cream, fresh salsa, and guacamole for a real fiesta. *Olé!*

* * * * *

1 Preheat the oven to 350°F. Coat a 9 x 13-inch casserole dish with cooking spray.

2 Bake the tortillas in a single layer on baking sheets for about 10 minutes or until crisp. Set aside to cool.

3 In a large skillet set over medium-high heat, combine the tomatoes and their juice, green onions, onion, salsa, and cumin. Bring to a boil, reduce the heat to low, and simmer, uncovered, for 8 minutes.

4 Stir in the soup and black beans, and cook 5 minutes or until heated through.

5 Spread one-third of the bean mixture over the bottom of the prepared casserole dish. Top with half of the tortillas, overlapping as necessary, and sprinkle over 1 cup of the cheese. Add another third of the bean mixture, top with the remaining tortillas, and sprinkle on 1 cup of the cheese.

Finish the layers with the last third of the bean mixture and remaining ½ cup cheese.

6 Bake the casserole for 25 to 30 minutes or until heated through, and serve hot.

Vegetarian friendly!

If you find yourself short on time, feel free to buy baked tortilla shells from the grocery store instead of toasting them yourself.

Sides That Take
Front and Center

Who can think of sides when they're overshadowed by gourmet delicacies? We can. Here are a whole bunch of lip-smacking, stick-to-your-ribs, make-them-go-"mmm" recipes that will leave everyone asking for more. Some recipes may play a support role, while others may try to steal the show. We've learned that the main course doesn't always have to be the main event. Inventive sides like our creamy Cauliflower Gratin (page 136), and our light (yet very flavorful) Herb-Baked Caprese Tomato Stacks (page 128), can transform mealtime standbys into real standouts. They're quick and easy, too—very desirable qualities for those cooks who have a gazillion other things to do besides cook. Enjoy a wide range of dishes that will bring the best to any occasion, including heaping portions of praise.

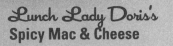

Lunch Lady Doris's
Spicy Mac & Cheese

Broccoli **Cornbread**

Green Rice *Hot Dish*

Onion Surprise *Casserole*

Herb-Baked **Caprese Tomato
Stacks**

Creamed Carrot Crunch *Casserole*

Oh Boy! **Broccoli Casserole**

A+ Asparagus

Sweet Potato *Casserole*

Cauliflower *Gratin*

Zucchini *Delight*

Rockin' **Tomatoes Rockefeller**

Rosemary Parmesan **Scalloped
Potatoes**

Cook Family **Pineapple Casserole**

Lunch Lady Doris's Spicy Mac & Cheese

MAKES 8 SERVINGS

1½ cups dried elbow macaroni

2½ cups fresh or frozen broccoli florets

½ cup sun-dried tomatoes

2 tablespoons unsalted butter

⅓ cup sliced green onions, green parts only

2 tablespoons all-purpose flour

2 teaspoons cayenne

1½ teaspoons dried basil

1 teaspoons salt

1¾ cups whole milk

6 ounces sharp Cheddar cheese, shredded (1½ cups)

4 ounces Gruyère cheese, grated (1 cup)

4 ounces Gouda cheese, grated (1 cup)

Who said macaroni and cheese is just for kids? It may have been during our adolescent days in the lunchroom where we fell in love with this all-American comfort dish, but this is *not* the macaroni and cheese of your childhood! Our version includes savory veggies, a rich medley of grown-up cheeses, and just enough cayenne to take this simple comfort food to a new gourmet delight. Makes a complete meal on its own or is a great side for just about anything, but we suggest serving it with some creamy tomato soup. Delish!

✳   ✳   ✳   ✳   ✳

1 Preheat the oven to 350°F.

2 Cook the macaroni according to package instructions. If you are using fresh broccoli, blanch in hot salted water for 5 minutes, then drain. If you are using frozen broccoli, thaw and drain it. Add the broccoli to the macaroni. Set aside.

3 Meanwhile, place the sun-dried tomatoes in a small bowl and add enough warm water to cover. Let stand for 10 minutes or until softened. Drain well, then chop into ¼-inch pieces and set aside.

4 Melt the butter in a medium saucepan set over medium heat. Add the green onions and cook until tender, about 5 minutes. Stir in the flour, cayenne, basil, and salt. Add the milk, and cook, stirring, until slightly thickened and bubbly. Add ¾ cup of the Cheddar, the Gruyère, and Gouda, a little at a time, stirring well after each addition, until the cheeses are melted. Stir in the macaroni and broccoli mixture and the softened sun-dried tomatoes. Transfer to

a 9 x 13-inch casserole dish and sprinkle the top of the casserole with the remaining ¾ cup Cheddar cheese.

5 Bake for about 30 minutes or until the cheese is melted and the casserole is heated through.

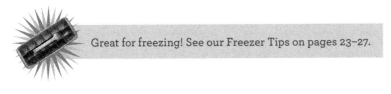
Great for freezing! See our Freezer Tips on pages 23–27.

Vegetarian friendly!

Broccoli Cornbread

MAKES 6 TO 8 SERVINGS

Cooking spray

2 (8½-ounce) boxes Jiffy cornbread mix

1½ cups cottage cheese

1 (10-ounce) box frozen broccoli cuts, thawed and well drained

¾ cup (1½ sticks) unsalted butter, melted

3 large eggs

¼ teaspoon salt

Sandy doesn't even like cornbread, and yet this is one of her favorite dishes. If you weren't one before, we'll make a cornbread lover out of you, too. This dish is extremely easy to make and works great when paired with our CQ's Royal Cottage Pie (page 38) or our Shrimply Delicious Shrimp and Grits (page 54). It also can stand proud all on its own, making a great appetizer or a replacement for the rolls in your bread basket!

1 Preheat the oven to 350°F. Lightly coat a 9 x 13-inch casserole dish with cooking spray.

2 Combine the cornbread mix, cottage cheese, broccoli, butter, eggs, and salt in a large bowl. Pour into the prepared casserole dish and bake for 30 minutes or until the center is firm and the top is golden brown.

Vegetarian friendly!

Green Rice Hot Dish

You betcha it's a hot dish! The history of the "hotdish" goes back to when budget-conscious farm wives needed to feed their own families as well as congregations of the first Minnesota churches. This filling side resembles a quiche and is packed full of flavor. Evaporated milk, which is thicker and richer than regular milk, helps give this dish its creamy texture. Perfect for cold winters, when you just need something warm and tasty in your belly.

✳ ✳ ✳ ✳ ✳

1 Preheat the oven to 350°F. Coat a 9 x 13-inch casserole dish with cooking spray.

2 Put the rice, cheese, evaporated milk, onion, parsley, eggs, garlic, olive oil, salt, and pepper into a large mixing bowl and stir well. Pour the mixture into the prepared casserole dish. Bake for 50 minutes or until the casserole is set and the top is brown and a little crunchy.

Vegetarian friendly!

MAKES 6 TO 8 SERVINGS

Cooking spray

2 cups cooked long-grain white rice (see page 195)

12 ounces sharp Cheddar cheese, grated (3 cups)

1 (12-ounce) can evaporated milk

1 medium onion, chopped

1 cup chopped fresh flat-leaf parsley

2 large eggs, beaten

1 garlic clove, minced

2 tablespoons olive oil

2 teaspoons salt

½ teaspoon freshly ground black pepper

Onion Surprise *Casserole*

MAKES 6 TO 8 SERVINGS

¼ cup plus 2 tablespoons
(¾ stick) unsalted butter

3 medium Texas 1015 onions or
3 Vidalia onions, chopped

8 ounces Swiss cheese, grated
(2 cups)

1 cup crushed saltine crackers

2 large eggs

¾ cup heavy cream

1 teaspoon salt

⅛ teaspoon freshly ground
black pepper

One day, when thumbing through her mom's recipe box, Sandy found this recipe from her Aunt Estelle. On the recipe card, Aunt Estelle had simply written the comment: "This is really good." Knowing the caliber of cook that Estelle is, Sandy and her mom decided to try it, even though an onion casserole didn't really sound like much. To their surprise, this is an absolutely amazing side dish.

This recipe features the delicious 1015 onion. Created in Weslaco (just down the road from where Sandy grew up) by Leonard Pike, at the Texas A&M University Extension Service, Texas 1015 onions are known for their mild, juicy, and sweet characteristics, as well as the fact that they contain very little pyruvate (the chemical that causes strong flavor and leads to tears). So, no more crying in the kitchen—cooking is supposed to be fun!

1 Preheat the oven to 350°F.

2 Melt ¼ cup (4 tablespoons) of the butter in a large skillet set over medium-high heat. Add the onions and sauté until tender and translucent, about 8 minutes. Put half of the onions into a 9 x 13-inch casserole dish. Sprinkle with 1 cup of the cheese and ½ cup of the cracker crumbs. Repeat the layers of onion and cheese.

3 In a medium bowl, lightly beat the eggs, then add the cream, salt, and pepper. Pour the mixture evenly over the casserole.

4 Melt the remaining 2 tablespoons of butter in a small skillet and stir in the remaining ½ cup cracker crumbs. Toast the crumbs until they are lightly brown, about 10 minutes, then sprinkle over the casserole.

5 Bake for 25 minutes, or until the onions have softened and the cracker crust is golden brown.

 Vegetarian friendly!

Herb-Baked Caprese Tomato Stacks

MAKES 8 SERVINGS

Cooking spray

3 medium tomatoes, cut into ¼-inch-thick slices

Salt and freshly ground black pepper

8 ¼-inch-thick slices fresh mozzarella

1 tablespoon chopped fresh basil

⅓ cup seasoned bread crumbs (see page 196)

2 teaspoons unsalted butter, melted

Vegetarian friendly!

This dish is so simply prepared, yet yields amazingly complex flavors. Sandy was inspired to make these tasty stacks from ingredients that seemed always to be on hand in her and Michael's home. Because there are so few ingredients in this dish, it is imperative that your ingredients are quality. We also recommend that you take the time to make your bread crumbs from scratch, as it adds that extra something to the dish. And don't worry about any extra bread crumbs getting stale; just store them in the freezer and they will stay fresh for months. If you find yourself with extra basil, don't waste it! Use it to make some tasty pesto (see opposite).

1 Preheat the oven to 425°F. Coat a 9 x 13-inch casserole dish with cooking spray.

2 Arrange one layer of tomatoes (do not overlap) in the bottom of the casserole dish. Season the tomatoes with salt and pepper. Put a slice of fresh mozzarella on top of each tomato, then top each with basil. Top each stack with another slice of tomato, and season with salt and pepper.

3 Combine the bread crumbs and butter in a small bowl. Sprinkle the crumbs over the stacks.

4 Bake for 5 to 10 minutes or until the tomatoes are heated through, the bread crumbs are lightly browned, and the mozzarella just starts to melt. Serve hot.

Pesto

When a recipe calls for just a bit of fresh basil, don't let the rest go to waste—in fact, buy a little extra (three bunches total) and make a delicious pesto. It's easy!

MAKES 1½ CUPS

4 large garlic cloves

¾ cup toasted pine nuts

¾ cup grated Parmesan cheese (3 ounces)

1½ teaspoons salt

½ teaspoon freshly ground black pepper

3 cups loosely packed fresh basil

⅔ cup extra-virgin olive oil

Place ingredients in a food processor and blend. If not using immediately, put the pesto in a zip-top plastic bag and freeze for up to 2 months.

Creamed Carrot Crunch *Casserole*

MAKES 6 TO 8 SERVINGS

Cooking spray

4 tablespoons (½ stick) unsalted butter

2 pounds carrots, peeled and cut into ¼-inch-thick pieces

1 tablespoon salt, plus more to taste

1 teaspoon freshly ground black pepper

½ teaspoon dried marjoram

2 tablespoons all-purpose flour

1½ cups heavy cream

3 medium garlic cloves, minced

1½ cups panko bread crumbs

 Vegetarian friendly!

Say that three times fast! It'll cook up even faster. This dish is easy to whip up, amazingly creamy and rich, and versatile. We particularly love it with our Damn Skinny Yankee Pot Roast (page 104) and our Tuna Noodle Casserole (page 53).

1 Preheat the oven to 350°F. Lightly coat a 9 x 13-inch casserole dish with cooking spray.

2 Melt 2 tablespoons of the butter in a large skillet set over medium-high heat. Add the carrots, salt, pepper, and marjoram. Cook, stirring occasionally, until the carrots just start to brown, about 7 minutes. Sprinkle the flour over the carrots, stirring constantly. Cook until flour turns golden, 1 to 2 minutes. Slowly pour in the cream while stirring constantly. Bring to a boil, then remove the pan from the heat.

3 Pour the mixture into the prepared casserole dish and cover with aluminum foil. Bake until the cream is bubbling and the carrots just give way when pierced with a knife, 20 to 25 minutes.

4 Meanwhile, melt the remaining 2 tablespoons of butter in a medium skillet set over medium heat. Add the garlic and cook until the butter just begins to brown, about 3 minutes. Add the bread crumbs and season with salt and pepper. Cook, stirring occasionally, until the bread crumbs are lightly browned, about 5 minutes. Transfer to a medium bowl and set aside.

5 When casserole has finished cooking, remove the foil and allow it to sit for about 10 minutes. Sprinkle the toasted bread crumbs evenly over the top before serving.

Oh Boy! Broccoli Casserole

Helping kids everywhere learn to love broccoli! This classic broccoli, cheese, and rice casserole will quickly become a favorite in your family. (Maybe they'll forget to complain about eating something green.)

✳ ✳ ✳ ✳ ✳

1 **Preheat the oven to 350°F. Coat a 2-quart casserole dish with cooking spray.**

2 **Combine 3 cups of the cooked rice, the broccoli, soup, cheese, onion, milk, and butter in a large bowl. Spoon the mixture into the prepared casserole dish. Bake for 45 minutes, or until the cheese has melted and the casserole is heated through.**

Great for freezing! See our Freezer Tips on pages 23–27.

Vegetarian friendly!

MAKES 6 TO 8 SERVINGS

Cooking spray

3 cups cooked long-grain white rice (see page 195)

2 (10-ounce) packages frozen chopped broccoli, thawed and drained

1 (10¾-ounce) can cream of mushroom soup, or 1½ cups homemade Cream of Mushroom Soup (page 203)

8 ounces Velveeta, diced, or Cheddar or Monterey jack, shredded (2 cups)

½ cup chopped onion

¼ cup whole milk

2 tablespoons unsalted butter, softened

A+ Asparagus

MAKES 6 TO 8 SERVINGS

Cooking spray

2 pounds fresh asparagus

7 tablespoons unsalted butter

2 shallots, minced

2 garlic cloves, minced

1 (12-ounce) jar marinated artichoke hearts, drained and rinsed

1 pound baby bella mushrooms, thickly sliced

½ teaspoon salt

½ teaspoon freshly ground black pepper

1 cup Ritz cracker crumbs

2 tablespoons all-purpose flour

1¾ cups heavy cream

¼ teaspoon cayenne

1 teaspoon smoked paprika

4 ounces Cheddar cheese, grated (1 cup)

Every Christmas, Crystal's family (the Cook side) gets together for a holiday party at her Aunt Mary Ann's. Since the family is so large, it's the one time of year that everyone makes the effort to be there to visit with one another. Everyone brings a dish for the buffet, and we all eat like kings and queens. Crystal's Aunt Sonja is known as one of the family's best cooks. Always aiming to impress her guests, she relies on this side dish to do just that. And if you ever thought asparagus was boring, you'll change your mind once you taste it all dolled up with shallots, artichokes, and baby portobella mushrooms. It's a real showstopper.

✳   ✳   ✳   ✳   ✳

1 Preheat the oven to 350°F. Coat a 9 x 13-inch casserole dish with cooking spray.

2 Hold an asparagus spear with both hands, about 2 inches from the ends. Gently bend the asparagus until it snaps. It will break at the point where the stem is too tough to be enjoyable; discard the stem. Repeat for all your asparagus. Cook the asparagus in boiling water until crisp tender, 2 to 3 minutes. Drain and set aside.

3 Melt 3 tablespoons of the butter in a medium sauté pan set over medium-high heat. Add the shallots and garlic, and sauté until soft, about 5 minutes. Add the artichoke hearts and mushrooms, and cook until tender, about 10 minutes. Season with ¼ teaspoon of the salt and ¼ teaspoon of the pepper. Set aside.

4 Melt 2 tablespoons of the butter in a small bowl. Add the cracker crumbs and stir well. Put three-quarters of the cracker crumbs into the prepared casserole dish. Spoon the artichoke mixture on top of the crumbs and top with the asparagus.

5 Melt the remaining 2 tablespoons of the butter in a saucepan set over medium heat. Add the flour and cook until it turns light brown and forms a paste. Slowly stir in the cream, cayenne, paprika, remaining ¼ teaspoon salt, and remaining ¼ teaspoon pepper. Cook, stirring, until the mixture thickens, about 10 minutes. Pour the sauce over the vegetables, and sprinkle with the cheese and the remaining cracker crumbs.

6 Bake 25 to 30 minutes or until the sauce is bubbly and the cheese is melted.

 Vegetarian friendly!

 Paprika is made from ground dried bell peppers or chiles. It can range from sweet to spicy, depending on the kind of pepper used. Smoked paprika is generally harder to find than regular mild paprika, but take it from Crystal—it's worth the effort. This dish benefits from the added rich, smoky flavor.

Sweet Potato Casserole

MAKES 6 TO 8 SERVINGS

8 large sweet potatoes

⅔ cup packed light brown sugar

⅔ cup pecans, toasted

½ cup all-purpose flour

5 tablespoons unsalted butter, plus more for greasing the casserole dish

¾ cup heavy cream

½ cup pure maple syrup

1 large egg, beaten

2 teaspoons vanilla extract

1 teaspoon salt

Wham bam, thank you, yam! Even if you've never been a sweet potato fan, you will love this seriously delicious casserole. No marshmallows needed here—brown sugar, pecans, and maple syrup make this dish so irresistibly tempting that seconds are rarely turned down.

1 Preheat the oven to 400°F.

2 Wash the sweet potatoes, dry well, and put on a baking sheet. Bake for about 1 hour or until soft. Remove the potatoes from the oven.

3 Reduce the oven temperature to 375°F.

4 Put the brown sugar, pecans, flour, and 5 tablespoons butter in the bowl of a food processor. Pulse until crumbly. Transfer the mixture to a bowl and put in the refrigerator until ready to use.

5 In the bowl of a stand mixer, fitted with the paddle attachment, add the cream, maple syrup, egg, vanilla, and salt. Peel the baked sweet potatoes, and add the flesh to the bowl. Beat the sweet potato mixture on medium-high speed until smooth.

6 Grease a 9 x 13-inch casserole dish with some butter. Pour the sweet potato mixture into the dish and smooth the top with the back of a spoon. Sprinkle the pecan topping evenly over the dish. Bake for 40 minutes or until heated through and the top has browned.

Vegetarian friendly!

To quickly toast nuts and seeds without your constant attention, place ¼ cup of nuts or seeds in a microwave dish and add 1 teaspoon butter. Microwave on high for about 5 minutes, stirring once after 2 minutes. While the nuts or seeds are toasting, you can be doing something else, like pouring yourself a glass of wine!

Cauliflower Gratin

MAKES 6 TO 8 SERVINGS

8 tablespoons (1 stick) unsalted butter

2 heads of cauliflower, cut into florets

Salt and freshly ground black pepper

½ cup finely chopped onion

2 garlic cloves, minced

½ cup all-purpose flour

3 cups whole milk

14 ounces Gruyère cheese, grated (3½ cups)

3 tablespoons chopped fresh flat-leaf parsley

⅔ cup panko bread crumbs

2 tablespoons chopped fresh chives

We even made cauliflower taste amazing. This dish is a standout, with roasted cauliflower smothered in a rich, creamy Gruyère sauce. The cauliflower develops a nice, deep browning from roasting that gives the gratin a fantastic sweet, nutty flavor. We like to serve this with our Charlotte's Prime Rib (page 72) or our Mandarin Meatloaf (page 103).

1 Preheat the oven to 400°F.

2 Melt 4 tablespoons of the butter. Put the cauliflower in a large roasting pan, drizzle the melted butter over the cauliflower, and toss well. Season liberally with salt, and roast in the oven for 30 minutes or until soft and slightly browned. Remove the pan from the oven, and set aside. Reduce the oven temperature to 350°F.

3 In a medium saucepan set over medium heat, melt 2 tablespoons of the butter. Add the onion and sauté until tender, about 8 minutes. Add the garlic and sauté for 1 minute. Add the flour and cook, whisking constantly, for 1 minute. Gradually add the milk while whisking constantly. Bring the mixture to a boil. Reduce the heat to low and simmer, stirring constantly, until the mixture has thickened, about 10 minutes.

4 Remove the pan from the heat, and add 2 cups of the Gruyère and the parsley. Stir until the cheese is melted and the sauce is smooth. Season with salt and pepper to taste. Add the roasted cauliflower and stir to coat. Pour the mixture into a 9 x 13-inch casserole dish.

5 Melt the remaining 2 tablespoons of the butter. In a small mixing bowl, combine the melted butter and the bread crumbs. Add the remaining 1½ cups cheese and the chives, and stir to combine. Sprinkle the topping evenly over the gratin.

6 Bake for 30 minutes or until bubbly and browned on top. Let the gratin cool for 10 minutes before serving.

 Vegetarian friendly!

Zucchini *Delight*

MAKES 6 TO 8 SERVINGS

Cooking spray

8 cups sliced zucchini (about 2½ pounds)

1 cup chopped onion

½ cup chicken broth (see page 200)

2 cups cooked long-grain white rice (see page 195)

1 cup sour cream

4 ounces sharp Cheddar cheese, shredded (1 cup)

¼ cup grated Parmesan cheese (1 ounce)

¼ cup seasoned bread crumbs (see page 196)

2 large eggs, lightly beaten

1 teaspoon salt

¼ teaspoon freshly ground black pepper

Our zucchini casserole tastes just as good as Mom's, but we've trimmed out many of the calories. Rich in flavor, this dish is a perfect partner for our Mamaw's Stuffed Peppers (page 58), Jayne's Baked Spaghetti (page 62), and Chicken Penne Pasta with Pink Sauce (page 74).

1 Preheat the oven to 350°F. Coat a 9 x 13-inch baking dish with cooking spray.

2 Combine the zucchini, onion, and chicken broth in a large pot set over medium-high heat, and bring to a boil. Cover, reduce the heat to low, and simmer for 20 minutes or until the vegetables are tender. Drain well, transfer to a large bowl, and partially mash the vegetables. Add the rice, sour cream, Cheddar cheese, 2 tablespoons of the Parmesan cheese, the bread crumbs, eggs, salt, and pepper to the vegetables, and stir gently to combine. Spoon the zucchini mixture into the prepared baking dish. Sprinkle the top with the remaining 2 tablespoons Parmesan cheese.

3 Bake for 30 minutes or until the top is golden brown.

 Great for freezing! See our Freezer Tips on pages 23–27.

 This dish can easily be made vegetarian by substituting vegetable broth for the chicken broth.

Tomatoes Rockefeller
Rockin'

The next time you have company, make sure to treat them to this! This relatively simple side will have your family and friends thinking you've cooked all day. And if you can get little Johnny to eat spinach, then that's a plus, too! This creamy, rich spinach dish graces the plate and stands up to any meat pairing, making it a perfect side for your next dinner party. When serving, use an ice cream scoop to make neat, perfectly shaped mounds. Try pairing it with our Savory Salmon Turnovers (page 90) or our Pastitsio (page 70).

Try pairing it with our Savory Salmon Turnovers (page 90) or our Pastitsio (page 70).

MAKES 6 TO 8 SERVINGS

Cooking spray

6 tablespoons (¾ stick) unsalted butter

1 medium onion, finely chopped

2 (10-ounce) packages frozen spinach, thawed and drained

1 cup lightly crushed herbed croutons

1 cup grated Parmesan cheese (4 ounces)

2 large eggs, beaten

2 teaspoons Tabasco sauce

1 teaspoon garlic powder

½ teaspoon salt, plus more to taste

½ teaspoon freshly ground black pepper, plus more to taste

2 large ripe tomatoes

1 Preheat the oven to 350°F. Coat a 9 x 13-inch casserole dish with cooking spray.

2 In a medium sauté pan set over medium heat, melt the butter. Add the onion and sauté for 8 minutes or until it starts to soften. Reduce the heat to low and add the spinach, croutons, ½ cup of the cheese, the eggs, Tabasco, garlic powder, salt, and pepper. Cook, stirring occasionally, for around 20 minutes, or until eggs are no longer runny.

3 Cut the tomatoes into six thick slices. Arrange the slices in the bottom of the prepared casserole dish. Season with salt and pepper. Bake the tomato slices for 8 to 10 minutes or until they begin to soften.

4 Preheat the broiler.

5 Divide the spinach mixture evenly over the tomato slices. Sprinkle the remaining ½ cup Parmesan on top of the spinach mixture. Return the casserole to the oven and broil for 2 minutes or until the cheese is golden brown. Serve immediately.

Vegetarian friendly!

Rosemary Parmesan Scalloped Potatoes

MAKES 8 TO 10 SERVINGS

¾ cup (1½ sticks) unsalted butter, plus more for greasing pan

3 to 4 pounds russet potatoes, peeled and in ⅛-inch-thick slices

1½ teaspoons salt

1½ teaspoons freshly ground black pepper

1½ teaspoons finely chopped fresh rosemary

3½ cups whole milk

1 cup grated Parmesan cheese (4 ounces)

There were certain food pairings in the Pollock house that never varied. When meatloaf was on the table, it was a given that these scalloped potatoes and green beans were faithfully by its side. No, maybe not a given—a guarantee, something you could bet the farm on. Today we serve these potatoes with more than just meatloaf. In fact, they're a great sidekick for Beef Burgundy (page 68) and our Coq au Vin (page 78).

❋ ❋ ❋ ❋ ❋

1 Preheat the oven to 350°F. Grease a 9 x 13-inch casserole dish with some butter.

2 Layer one-third of the potato slices in the bottom of the casserole dish, overlapping slightly, so that the dish is completely covered. Dot the top of the potatoes with 4 tablespoons of the butter, then season with ½ teaspoon of the salt, ½ teaspoon of the pepper, and ½ teaspoon of the rosemary. Repeat these layers two more times. Pour the milk over the top of the potatoes.

3 Place the casserole dish in the oven and bake for 1 hour. Remove from the oven and evenly sprinkle the Parmesan cheese over the potatoes. Bake for 30 more minutes or until the top is golden brown and the potatoes can be pierced with a knife easily.

Vegetarian friendly!

Cook Family Pineapple Casserole

Sounds strange, but it is really delicious. (Crystal had to convince Sandy, too.) There's something about the sweet-salty combination of pineapple, Cheddar cheese, and Ritz crackers that's irresistible. This casserole is generally served as a side, but it's sweet enough for dessert.

* * * * *

1 Preheat the oven to 350°F. Lightly coat a 9 x 13-inch casserole dish with cooking spray.

2 In a medium bowl, combine the flour and sugar. Drain the pineapple, reserving 6 tablespoons of the juice. Add the juice to the flour and sugar, and stir to combine. Add the pineapple and cheese. Stir well, and pour into the prepared casserole dish.

3 In a separate bowl, combine the cracker crumbs and butter. Sprinkle the crumbs on top of the casserole. Bake for 20 to 30 minutes or until the crumb topping is golden brown and the casserole is heated through.

 Vegetarian friendly!

MAKES 6 TO 8 SERVINGS

Cooking spray

6 tablespoons all-purpose flour

1 cup sugar

2 (20-ounce) cans unsweetened pineapple chunks

8 ounces mild Cheddar cheese, grated (2 cups)

1 roll Ritz crackers, crushed

¾ cup (1½ sticks) unsalted butter, melted

Rise and Shine! Casseroles to Start the Day

For the majority of us, breakfast doesn't play a big enough role in our busy and hectic lifestyles. And if we do find the time in our morning schedules, it sadly consists of a cup of coffee and a bowl of cold cereal. (Shame, shame!) For us, breakfast really is the most important meal of the day—and it's one that should be fully appreciated and enjoyed. With these easy casserole recipes—and a few make-ahead ones, too—breakfast can be something special, as it should be. So whether you're planning a brunch get-together with friends or just want to surprise the kids, here are some tried-and-true recipes that will have them jumping out of bed in no time. Sweet or savory, these delightful dishes are not your average breakfast fare. They make breakfast a brighter occasion and could just turn you into a morning person.

Frenchy Toast Casserole

Citrus Blintz

Bed and Breakfast Casserole

Smokin' Strata

Texas Migas

The "Pile High" Frittata

Sunday's Best Crab and
Cheese Quiche

A Side of Hash Brown Casserole,
Please!

Ham and Cheese Skillet
Casserole

Not-Just-for-Breakfast
Garlic Cheese Grits

Granola Oatmeal Bake

Caramel Cinnamon Sweet Rolls

Blueberry Coffee Cake

Freakin' Insane Chocolate-
Chip Applesauce Quick Bread

Crescent Roll Casserole

Frenchy Toast *Casserole*

MAKES 6 TO 8 SERVINGS

¾ cup (1½ sticks) unsalted butter

1½ cups packed light brown sugar

2 teaspoons ground cinnamon

1 loaf extra-thick sliced white bread, such as Texas Toast, crusts removed

2 cups whole milk

6 large eggs

1 cup your favorite berries

There are no grumpy faces when it's a Frenchy Toast Casserole morning. This dish puts the "sweet" in "home sweet home." Add your kids' favorite berries, and you've got yourself one tasty treat.

1 Preheat the oven to 350°F.

2 Melt the butter in a small saucepan set over medium heat. Add the brown sugar and 1 teaspoon of the cinnamon and stir to make a paste. Spread the paste in the bottom of a 9 x 13-inch casserole dish. Lay the bread on top of the paste in two layers.

3 In a separate bowl, combine the milk, eggs, and remaining 1 teaspoon cinnamon. Pour the mixture over the bread in the dish. Bake for 30 minutes, or until top has risen a little and is golden brown. Top with berries when serving.

Great for freezing! See our Freezer Tips on pages 23–27.

This casserole can be made the night before and kept chilled in the fridge overnight. All you'll have to do the next morning is pop it in the oven.

Vegetarian friendly!

CQ's Royal
Cottage Pie PAGE 38

Deep-Dish Pizza,
Chicago Style PAGE 46

World's Greatest
Chicken Pot Pie
PAGE 48

Valley-Style
Arroz con Pollo PAGE 50

Shrimply Delicious
Shrimp and Grits PAGE 54

Rosemary Parmesan
Scalloped Potatoes
PAGE 140

Beef Burgundy
PAGE 68

Mamaw's Stuffed Peppers
PAGE 58

Sweet Potato
Casserole PAGE 134

Charlotte's
Prime Rib PAGE 72

Oh Boy!
Broccoli Casserole
PAGE 131

A+ Asparagus
PAGE 132

Savory Salmon Turnovers
PAGE 90

Red Snapper
Veracruz PAGE 116

Black Bean
Enchilada Casserole
PAGE 118

Herb-Baked
Caprese Tomato Stacks
PAGE 128

Frenchy Toast
Casserole PAGE 144

Blueberry Coffee Cake
PAGE 160

Smokin' Strata
PAGE 147

Pollock's Peach Cobbler
PAGE 179

Peanut Butter Freezer Pie with
Chocolate and Bananas
PAGE 182

Citrus Blintz

The area where Sandy grew up in the Rio Grande Valley is one of the best places in the nation for growing citrus. There is something about the soil, climate, and constant sunshine that lends itself to perfect citrus farming. Sandy's dad Max worked the citrus farms, and every year Sandy would go out with her dad to the farms to help him harvest and to sample the goods! It's only natural that when developing recipes, Sandy wanted to pull from this fond memory. This wonderfully delicious spin on traditional blintzes has all the great taste but without all the work. Forget the trial and error; use this surefire recipe to woo your crowd.

1 Preheat the oven to 350°F. Coat a 9 x 13-inch casserole dish with cooking spray.

2 In a blender, combine the eggs, egg whites, sour cream, grapefruit zest, orange juice, and butter. Cover and blend until smooth. Add the flour, ½ cup of the sugar, and the baking powder. Cover and blend again until smooth. Transfer the batter to a medium bowl.

3 In a clean blender, combine the cottage cheese, cream cheese, egg yolks, vanilla, lemon juice, and remaining 2 tablespoons sugar. Cover and blend until smooth.

4 Pour 2 cups of the batter into the prepared casserole dish. Spoon the cottage cheese mixture over the batter and swirl the filling into the batter with the tip of a knife. Pour the remaining batter evenly over the mixture in the dish. Bake for 45 minutes or until puffed and golden. Cool for 30 minutes on a wire rack before serving.

5 To serve, heat the marmalade with the water in a small saucepan set over medium heat until melted. Drizzle the blintz with the melted marmalade and spread to cover.

MAKES 8 TO 10 SERVINGS

Cooking spray

6 large eggs

2 egg whites

1½ cups sour cream

2 teaspoons finely grated grapefruit zest

½ cup fresh orange juice

¼ cup (½ stick) unsalted butter, softened

1 cup all-purpose flour

½ cup plus 2 tablespoons sugar

2 teaspoons baking powder

2 cups cottage cheese

1 (8-ounce) package cream cheese, softened

2 egg yolks

2 teaspoons vanilla extract

1 teaspoon fresh lemon juice

½ cup orange marmalade

2 tablespoons water

Bed and Breakfast *Casserole*

MAKES 6 TO 8 SERVINGS

Cooking spray

1 (8-ounce) round Brie cheese

1 pound ground hot pork sausage

12 slices thin white bread, crusts removed

1½ cups grated Parmesan cheese (6 ounces)

7 large eggs

3 cups heavy cream

2 cups whole milk

1½ tablespoons dried sage

1½ teaspoons dry mustard

1 teaspoon seasoned salt

This casserole can be made the night before and kept chilled in the fridge overnight, so all you have to do the next morning is pop it in the oven.

Bed and breakfast inns are very popular in the areas surrounding Austin, Texas, which is known as the "Hill Country." Around here, B&Bs are usually historic homes that have been in the innkeepers' families for years. One of the best aspects of staying at a B&B is breakfast! The innkeeper traditionally gets up early and prepares a lovely morning spread for the guests. The richness of Brie, sausage, and egg reminds us of days well spent relaxing around a perfect breakfast with other guests at our favorite B&Bs.

1 Preheat the oven to 350°F. Lightly coat a 9 x 13-inch casserole with cooking spray.

2 Trim the rind from the Brie. (Place the cheese in the freezer for about 30 minutes before trimming to make it easier to work with.) Cut the cheese into ¼-inch cubes; set aside.

3 Cook the sausage in a large skillet set over medium-high heat, breaking up any lumps with the back of a spoon, until browned throughout, about 6 minutes. Drain well.

4 Layer the bread in the bottom of the prepared casserole dish. Scatter the sausage, Brie, and Parmesan cheese over the bread.

5 In a large bowl, lightly whisk the eggs, then add the cream, milk, sage, dry mustard, and seasoned salt. Whisk to combine and pour evenly over the casserole. Bake for 50 minutes, or until the egg mixture is set. Serve hot.

Great for freezing! See our Freezer Tips on pages 23–27.

Smokin' Strata

In the words of Crystal's dad, Jody, "Sometimes you just want breakfast for dinner." We couldn't agree more. This egg masterpiece is not only great for breakfast but also ideal for a savory dinner any night of the week. Aside from the taste, the beautiful thing about stratas is how filling they are. At the heart of any great strata you will find a dense, rustic bread (we use focaccia) layered with an egg mixture and cheese. In this particular recipe we add leeks and red bell peppers for a touch of sweetness and color, but the real standout is the smoky flavor provided by the Gouda cheese. Hence, the strata's name. Enjoy!

MAKES 6 TO 8 SERVINGS

Cooking spray

2 tablespoons unsalted butter

1½ medium red bell peppers, finely chopped

2 leeks, thinly sliced, white and light green parts only

1 (10-ounce) loaf focaccia bread, cut into ½-inch cubes

4 ounces mild smoked Gouda cheese, grated (1 cup)

1½ cups whole milk

1½ cups half-and-half

9 large eggs, lightly beaten

2 tablespoons Dijon mustard

½ teaspoon salt

½ teaspoon freshly ground black pepper

1 Preheat oven to 375°F. Coat a 9 x 13-inch casserole dish with cooking spray.

2 In a medium sauté pan set over medium-high heat, melt the butter. Add the bell peppers and leeks and sauté until soft, about 8 minutes. Set aside.

3 Spread half of the bread cubes in the prepared casserole dish. Top with three-fourths of the cheese and three-fourths of the red pepper mixture. Repeat the layers.

4 In a medium bowl, whisk together the milk, half-and-half, eggs, mustard, salt, and pepper. Pour over the strata layers. Bake for 1 hour, or until the eggs are firm and set in the center and the top of the casserole is golden brown.

Vegetarian friendly!

Texas Migas

MAKES 8 TO 10 SERVINGS

Cooking spray

6 corn tortillas

Vegetable oil, for frying

12 large eggs

2 tablespoons heavy cream

¼ cup (½ stick) unsalted butter

½ cup chopped onion

1 cup chopped green bell pepper

1 (10-ounce) can Rotel tomatoes or diced tomatoes with green chiles

¼ cup chopped fresh cilantro

1 teaspoon salt

1 teaspoon freshly ground black pepper

¼ cup chopped pickled jalapeño peppers

8 ounces Cheddar or Monterey jack, grated (2 cups)

Vegetarian friendly!

If you have ever had breakfast in Texas, then odds are you've experienced a plate of delicious migas, a mixture of fluffy eggs, spices, cheese, and fried tortillas. For Sandy, migas present somewhat of a love-hate relationship. You see, Michael (her main squeeze for over twelve years) loves migas so much she sometimes feels he loves them more than her. He's tried them in every restaurant in Austin, always noting the subtle differences and what would make the perfect combination of flavors. She took note and developed this recipe in attempts of satisfying her "migas man." And let's just say there is no longer any doubt who Michael loves more. Serve these with a side of refried beans and your choice of corn, flour, or whole wheat tortillas to enfold all of the ingredients into tasty tacos. And if you're feeling spicy, try making your own pickled jalapeños (see opposite).

1 Preheat the oven to 350°F. Coat a 9 x 13-inch casserole dish with cooking spray.

2 Cut the tortillas into ¼-inch-thick strips. Heat the vegetable oil in a wide skillet set over medium-high heat until it reaches 350°F on a deep-fry thermometer. Working in small batches, lay the tortilla strips in the oil and fry, turning occasionally, for about 1 minute. Look for the strips to become golden brown and crunchy. Remove the strips from the oil and let drain on a paper towel. Set aside.

3 In a large bowl, whisk together the eggs and cream. Set aside.

4 In a medium sauté pan set over medium-high heat, melt the butter. Add the onion and bell pepper, and sauté until the onion is translucent and the pepper starts to soften, about 8 minutes. Transfer the mixture to the bowl with the eggs, then add the tomatoes, cilantro, salt, and pepper. Mix well.

5 Pour the egg mixture into the prepared casserole dish. Place the casserole in the oven and bake for 30 minutes, or until the eggs are just set in the center. Remove the casserole from the oven and sprinkle the jalapeños, cheese, and fried tortilla strips evenly over the top. Return the casserole to the oven and continue to cook for 5 to 8 minutes or until the cheese melts. Remove from the oven and let sit for 5 minutes before serving.

Pickled Jalapeños

MAKES 3 PINTS

2 pounds fresh jalapeño peppers

5 cups white vinegar

4 teaspoons pickling salt

2 teaspoons sugar

Wash the peppers and cut them into ¼-inch-thick slices. Tightly pack the jalapeños into 3 pint jars, being careful not to crush them. Set aside.

In a medium saucepan, combine the vinegar, salt, and sugar with 1 cup of water. Bring the mixture to a boil over high heat and pour it over the peppers in the jars. Clean the rim of the jars with a clean towel and screw the canning lids securely on the jars. Process pints in a boiling water bath for 10 minutes. Place the jars in large pot and add enough water to cover the jars by 1 to 2 inches. Cover the pot and bring the water to a boil. Boil for 10 minutes. Turn off the heat, then carefully lift the jars out of the water and place on an absorbent towel. Let the jars cool completely. They can be stored for up to one year.

The "Pile High" Frittata

MAKES 6 TO 8 SERVINGS

3 tablespoons unsalted butter, plus more for pan

3 tablespoons canola oil

4 cups frozen shredded hash brown potatoes

1 medium onion, thinly sliced

½ cup chopped green bell pepper

1 cup sliced green onions

⅛ teaspoon cayenne

2 teaspoons seasoning salt

Freshly ground black pepper

1 pound cooked ham, cubed

12 large eggs

¼ cup heavy cream

Pinch of Italian seasoning

8 ounces sharp Cheddar cheese, grated (2 cups)

Ever had a Denver omelet? If not, you are missing out on a real treat. A Denver omelet (sometimes also referred to as a western omelet) is a tasty egg concoction typically prepared with Cheddar cheese, diced ham, onions, green bell peppers, and sometimes scattered hash browns. Its origins remain as scattered as the hash browns, but our best guess is that it probably originated one morning out on the range, cooked up by some hungry cowboys trying to fill their bellies. Inspired by their tasty creation, this recipe is the Queens' Casserole version of the popular dish. Pile your diced ham, green bell peppers, onions, cheese, and hash browns a mile high and watch it bake to a beautiful golden brown. We added a kick of cayenne pepper to spice it up a bit.

1 Place an oven rack in the bottom third of the oven. Preheat the oven to 375°F. Grease a 9 x 13-inch casserole dish with butter.

2 Heat the oil and 3 tablespoons butter in a skillet set over medium heat. Add the potatoes, onion, bell pepper, green onions, cayenne, 1 teaspoon of the seasoned salt, and black pepper to taste. Cook for about 8 minutes or until the vegetables are very lightly browned. Add the ham and cook for 3 more minutes, stirring every once in a while with a wooden spoon or spatula. Transfer the mixture to the prepared baking dish.

3 In a bowl, whisk together the eggs, cream, Italian seasoning, and remaining 1 teaspoon seasoned salt. Pour the egg mixture into the baking dish and toss with the potatoes. Bake for 25 minutes. Sprinkle the top of the casserole with the cheese, and bake for 8 to 10 minutes more, until the cheese is melted and the eggs are set. Cool for about 10 minutes before serving.

Did you know that green bell peppers are just immature red bell peppers? Well, neither did we—until Sandy discovered this fact. Green and red bell peppers have the same caloric content, but due to a longer maturation time, the red bells have much higher levels of vitamin C (almost twice as much) and tons more beta-carotene! So, if you are feeling low on vitamin C, feel free to substitute your green bell with a nutrition-packed red!

Sunday's Best
Crab and Cheese Quiche

MAKES 8 SERVINGS

2 large eggs, lightly beaten

½ cup whole milk

½ cup mayonnaise

1 teaspoon cornstarch

½ teaspoon smoked paprika

½ teaspoon salt

½ teaspoon freshly ground black pepper

½ pound lump crab meat, flaked

6 ounces Swiss cheese, shredded (1½ cups)

1 9-inch unbaked pie crust (see page 192)

Dress up this quiche and show it off for breakfast. Yes, we're talking about *your* quiche. You dress yourself in your Sunday best, so why not dress up your breakfast? Don't be fooled by its outer appearance; this quiche will surprise and delight as your family and guests discover surprising ingredients, such as fresh crab and smoked paprika, in their first bite.

❋ ❋ ❋ ❋ ❋

1 Preheat the oven to 350°F.

2 In a medium bowl, combine the eggs, milk, mayonnaise, cornstarch, paprika, salt, and pepper. Stir in the crab and cheese. Pour the mixture into the pie shell. Bake for 30 to 40 minutes, or until a knife inserted into center of the quiche comes out clean.

A Side of Hash Brown Casserole, *Please!*

Your morning eggs will find their perfect partner in this cheesy and delicious casserole. It's baked with a crunchy, buttery topping that will bring you back for seconds—and thirds! This casserole is a good alternative to mashed or baked potatoes at dinnertime, too. Try serving it with fried chicken for a true comfort feast.

1 Preheat oven to 350°F. Lightly coat a 9 x 13-inch casserole dish with cooking spray.

2 In a large bowl, combine the hash browns, ½ cup of the melted butter, the soup, sour cream, onion, cheese, salt, and pepper. Spoon the mixture into the prepared casserole dish.

3 In a medium saucepan set over medium heat, sauté the cornflake crumbs in the remaining ¼ cup melted butter until the cornflakes start to brown, about 4 minutes. Sprinkle the cornflakes over the top of the casserole. Cover the casserole with foil and bake for 40 minutes or until the top is golden brown and the edges are bubbling. Serve immediately.

MAKES 6 TO 8 SERVINGS

Cooking spray

1 (2-pound) package frozen hash brown potatoes, thawed

¾ cup (1½ sticks) unsalted butter, melted

1 (10¾-ounce) can cream of chicken soup, or 1½ cups homemade Cream of Chicken Soup (page 202)

1 (8-ounce) container sour cream

½ cup chopped onion

8 ounces Cheddar cheese, shredded (2 cups)

1 teaspoon salt

¼ teaspoon freshly ground black pepper

2 cups crushed cornflake cereal

If you want to freeze your casserole, don't include the cornflake topping. Save it to add right before baking so that it is extra crunchy!

This dish can be made vegetarian by using cream of mushroom soup instead of chicken soup. Now, isn't that easy?

Ham and Cheese
Skillet Casserole

MAKES 6 TO 8 SERVINGS

1 large russet potato, peeled and cut into ½-inch pieces

2 tablespoons vegetable oil

1 teaspoon salt

½ teaspoon freshly ground black pepper

2 large eggs

1 cup whole milk

1 tablespoon unsalted butter, melted

1 cup all-purpose flour

2 green onions, thinly sliced, green parts only

12 ounces thick-sliced deli ham, cut into ½-inch pieces

2 ounces sharp Cheddar cheese, shredded (½ cup)

One of the very few items Crystal has of her Mamaw Maggie's is her cast-iron skillet. Until recently she used the skillet only for making cornbread, but she has now discovered the pan's varied talents. If you are not familiar with cast-iron pans, they can seem intimidating. All that talk of properly seasoning them, how to wash them (or not wash), seems like too much work. But trust us, the benefits of the cast-iron pan far outweigh any care concerns. They heat evenly and beautifully, and when properly cared for, they will last a lifetime. Crystal's pan has lasted several lifetimes! This breakfast recipe will work with any oven-safe skillet, but when using a cast-iron skillet, your bottom layer of potatoes will get a nice crispness to it.

✳ ✳ ✳ ✳ ✳

1 Place an oven rack in the upper third of the oven. Preheat the oven to 450°F.

2 Toss the potatoes with 1 tablespoon of the vegetable oil, ¼ teaspoon of the salt, and ¼ teaspoon of pepper in a microwave-safe bowl. Cover the bowl with a paper towel and microwave on high, stirring the potatoes halfway through cooking, until the potatoes begin to soften, 5 to 7 minutes. Drain the potatoes well and set aside.

3 In a separate large bowl, whisk together the eggs, milk, butter, remaining ½ teaspoon of salt, and ¼ teaspoon of pepper. Stir in the flour and green onions until just incorporated but still a bit lumpy, and set aside.

4 Heat the remaining 1 tablespoon of oil in a 10-inch oven-safe skillet set over medium-high heat until shimmering. Add the ham and potatoes; cover the skillet with foil and

cook until the potatoes start to brown, about 10 minutes. Uncover the skillet, pour in the egg mixture, and sprinkle the cheese over the top. Bake for 25 to 30 minutes, or until puffed and golden. Transfer the skillet to a wire rack and let cool for 5 minutes. Use a rubber spatula to loosen the casserole from the skillet, then slide it onto a cutting board, slice into wedges, and serve.

If you decide to invest in a cast-iron skillet, here are Crystal's tips on how to properly season and store your pan. When properly seasoned, a cast-iron skillet works better than any nonstick pan around!

- Preheat the oven to 400°F.
- New pans will contain a coating of wax. Thoroughly wash the inside of your skillet with warm soapy water to remove the coating. Never put your cast-iron pan in the dishwasher or let it soak for any length of time.
- Important: Dry your skillet thoroughly with paper towels. It is imperative that it is completely dry. Do not let it air-dry.
- Dampen a paper towel with vegetable oil such as canola oil, or shortening such as Crisco, and wipe the inside of your skillet thoroughly, creating a nice sheen or glisten on the pan.

- Cover the bottom of your pan with coarse salt to a depth of about ½ inch up the sides of the pan.
- Place your skillet in the oven for 30 minutes.
- Using oven mitts, remove the pan from the oven. Place pan on a safe surface for cooling. Cool for 30 minutes or more until the pan is cool to the touch.
- Dump the salt from your skillet and wash the skillet with warm soapy water. Rinse and dry skillet thoroughly, as mentioned above.
- Before putting your pan away, be sure to give it another light coating of oil or shortening to protect it from rust and corrosion.

Not-Just-for-Breakfast Garlic Cheese Grits

MAKES 6 TO 8 SERVINGS

Cooking spray

Salt and freshly ground black pepper

4 garlic cloves, minced

2 cups quick-cooking grits

8 ounces sharp Cheddar cheese, grated (2 cups)

4 large eggs, beaten

20 dashes Tabasco sauce

Vegetarian friendly!

Some things are like clockwork. For Crystal, her weekly routine during her high school years consisted of getting up and making herself grits and toast for breakfast. Oh, how she loved her grits! Some mornings she had them with sugar and butter; other days she simply salt-and-peppered them. It didn't really matter how they were prepared. You can imagine, then, how sad she was when she couldn't find grits while at college in Boston (that and her sweet tea). Determined to get her college friends on track, Crystal had her mother ship her care packages loaded with containers of grits. She served them at every opportunity and explored different ways of preparing them in order to impress her guests. One of the most popular recipes was this delicious take, which adds the right amount of garlic and cheese. Forget cold cereal—mornings should be all about grits.

1 Preheat the oven to 375°F. Coat a 9 x 13-inch baking dish with cooking spray.

2 Bring 8 cups of water, 2 teaspoons salt, and garlic to a boil in a medium saucepan set over high heat. Once boiling, gradually add the grits, whisking constantly to break up any lumps. Reduce the heat to a simmer and cook, stirring occasionally, for 10 minutes, until the grits are thick.

3 Remove the pan from the heat and stir in 1½ cups of the cheese and the eggs. Add the Tabasco (less if you are not a fan of heat) and salt and pepper to taste. Pour the grits into the prepared baking dish. Bake for 45 minutes.

4 Sprinkle the remaining ½ cup cheese over the top, and bake for 15 more minutes, or until the grits are set and the cheese on top is melted. Let rest for 10 minutes before serving.

Granola Oatmeal Bake

Oatmeal is one of the healthiest and most energy-packed breakfast foods around. To give our loved ones a great start to their day while keeping a lazy weekend morning—well—lazy, we created this casserole. The three kinds of dried fruit and touch of vanilla dress it up just enough so that it still feels like a treat.

1 Preheat the oven to 350°F. Lightly coat a 9 x 13-inch casserole dish with cooking spray.

2 In a medium saucepan set over medium heat, bring the milk and butter to a boil. Slowly stir in the oats, apricots, cherries, golden raisins, 3 tablespoons of the brown sugar, the vanilla, and salt. Cook, stirring, for 1 minute. Pour the mixture into the prepared casserole dish.

3 Bake for 15 minutes. Sprinkle with the remaining 2 tablespoons brown sugar and the walnuts. Bake for 5 more minutes, or until bubbly. Cool slightly before serving.

MAKES 6 TO 8 SERVINGS

Cooking spray

1¾ cups whole milk

2 tablespoons unsalted butter

1 cup old-fashioned rolled oats

⅓ cup chopped dried apricots

⅓ cup dried tart cherries

⅓ cup golden raisins

5 tablespoons packed light brown sugar

½ teaspoon vanilla extract

¼ teaspoon salt

½ cup coarsely chopped walnuts

Caramel Cinnamon Sweet Rolls

MAKES 12 SERVINGS

1 package active dry yeast (2½ teaspoons)

¾ cup warm water

½ cup (1 stick) plus 2 table-spoons unsalted butter, softened

2¼ cups self-rising flour

1¼ cups plus 3 tablespoons sugar

1 large egg

1½ teaspoons ground cinnamon

Caramel Sauce (recipe follows)

Anyone would get right out of bed if he or she smelled these rolls rising in the oven—even on a Saturday! We believe the magic lies in the homemade caramel sauce. The caramel is rarely something we consider making from scratch, yet it is surprisingly easy to do. Double the sauce recipe and store the extra goodness in a plastic squeeze bottle in the fridge. The squeeze bottle is the perfect tool for drizzling this rich caramel over ice cream or apple slices.

✳   ✳   ✳   ✳   ✳

1 In the bowl of an electric mixer fitted with a paddle attach-ment, dissolve the yeast in the warm water. Add ½ cup of butter, 1 cup of the flour, 1¼ cups of the sugar, and the egg to the bowl. Beat for 2 minutes, then add the remaining 1¼ cups of flour and beat until smooth, about 2 minutes. Scrape the batter from the sides of the bowl. Transfer the dough to a clean bowl. Cover the bowl with a clean kitchen towel and let the dough rise in a warm place (about 85°F) until doubled in size, about 1 hour.

2 Turn the dough out onto a well-floured counter. Roll into a 9 x 12-inch rectangle. Gently spread 1 tablespoon of softened butter on the dough. In a small bowl, combine the cinnamon and remaining 3 tablespoons sugar; sprinkle onto the dough, leaving a ½-inch border around the dough. Roll the dough up like a jelly roll, starting from the larger side. Cut the dough into 12 equal pieces.

3 Place the rolls in a 9 x 13-inch casserole dish that has been greased with the other tablespoon of softened butter, tucking the loose ends of the dough under each roll so they'll hold together when baked. Cover the pan with a

clean kitchen towel and let the rolls rise in a warm place (about 85°F) until doubled in size, about 1 hour.

4 Preheat the oven to 350°F. Bake the rolls for 15 to 20 minutes, or until light golden brown. Brush the hot caramel sauce on the rolls while still hot.

Caramel Sauce

In a large pot set over medium-high heat, melt the butter. Add the brown sugar, granulated sugar, and honey. Bring to a boil, and cook for 4 to 5 minutes, stirring once or twice (watch carefully to avoid scorching). Remove the pot from the heat and swirl in the cream until it is fully incorporated. Be very careful when adding the cream because the mixture will bubble up.

MAKES 2 CUPS

1 cup (2 sticks) unsalted butter

1 cup packed light brown sugar

¼ cup granulated sugar

¾ cup honey

¼ cup heavy cream

Sandy's Granny Haley made the best cinnamon rolls in the world. It seemed so effortless and magical to her grandkids. The smell the cinnamon wafting through the house stopped people in their tracks. As Sandy grew older and really began to appreciate the lessons given her by her family, she started taking note when Granny would cook. Unfortunately for Sandy, one of her biggest regrets was not getting the exact measurements for the cinnamon rolls. When Sandy graduated from culinary school, one of the first tasks given to her by her mother was to re-create Granny's cinnamon rolls. Sandy was able to locate an old hand-written recipe card with the general method, but the problem was that the recipe said things like a "drop" of this and a "handful" of that. Sandy has worked diligently on these cinnamon rolls. She feels like hers have gotten really close to Granny's, but she thinks Granny's hands must have been much smaller. Her laughter and tiny hands are missed.

Blueberry Coffee Cake

MAKES 6 TO 8 SERVINGS

Cooking spray

2 cups all-purpose flour

1 cup granulated sugar

2 teaspoons baking powder

1½ teaspoons grated lemon zest

1 teaspoon salt

½ cup (1 stick) unsalted butter, softened

1 cup plus 3 to 5 teaspoons whole milk

2 large eggs, slightly beaten

1 teaspoon vanilla extract

1½ cups fresh or thawed frozen blueberries

1 cup confectioners' sugar

¼ teaspoon almond extract

Ever heard of "loafering"? Obviously, this is a Southern version of "loafing," a favorite Sunday afternoon occupation. "Loafering" was a term used often in Crystal's childhood—a word Crystal's mom used to describe their Sunday afternoon drives and visits with friends and family. Every Sunday, Crystal would climb into the family car with her mom and off they would go. One of their favorite stops was at Crystal's Great Aunt Cricket and Aunt Doc's house. (Yep, that is not a typo. When Crystal was a tiny red-haired child, she mistakenly called her Great Uncle Doc "Aunt Doc," and it stuck! Everyone called him Aunt Doc, and he didn't mind at all!) Aunt Cricket was the epitome of the Southern hostess, and she always had a pot of coffee brewed and a freshly baked cake on hand. The family would sit around her kitchen table and listen to Aunt Doc tell his outrageous stories, and the cake would always make the tales that much sweeter. This blueberry cake reminds Crystal of those afternoons and "loafering" around with her mom!

1 Preheat the oven to 375°F. Coat a 9 x 13-inch baking dish with cooking spray.

2 In a large bowl, combine the flour, granulated sugar, baking powder, lemon zest, and salt. Using pastry blender or fork, cut in the butter until the mixture resembles coarse crumbs. Add 1 cup of the milk, the eggs, and vanilla, and stir well. Pour three-fourths of the batter into the prepared pan. Top with the blueberries, then spoon the remaining batter over the blueberries. Bake for 35 minutes, until toothpick when inserted in the center of the cake comes out clean. Transfer to a wire rack and let cool 30 minutes.

3 In small bowl, whisk together the confectioners' sugar, almond extract, and 3 tablespoons of the milk. Add more milk as needed for the icing to be thin and easy to drizzle. Drizzle over the cake. Cut into squares and serve.

 Maybe blueberries aren't your thing. If that is the case, simply substitute with your favorite berry. Sandy loves making this recipe with blackberries and cherries, too. It really just depends on what is in season and what mood you're in!

Freakin' Insane Chocolate-Chip Applesauce Quick Bread

MAKES 6 TO 8 SERVINGS

Vegetable shortening, such as Crisco

2 cups all-purpose flour, plus more for dusting the pan

1½ cups applesauce

½ cup (1 stick) unsalted butter, melted

1 teaspoon vanilla extract

1 cup sugar

2 teaspoons baking soda

1 teaspoon ground allspice

1 teaspoon ground cloves

1 teaspoon ground cinnamon

½ teaspoon salt

1 cup semi-sweet chocolate chips

This outrageous breakfast bread was introduced to Crystal when she was at her dear friend Amy's home. It was one of those scenarios where you have room for only one piece, yet end up taking the loaf home! Amy told Crystal that her mom and her mom's friend Janie made this recipe often when Amy was growing up. When they had passed, Amy inherited her mom's recipe book, which included several copies of this recipe, in both her mom's and Janie's handwritings. Amy has taken to making it every holiday for her family and friends. Baking and sharing this delicious bread with the rest of the family is the ultimate way to honor their memories and their special friendship.

✳ ✳ ✳ ✳ ✳

1 Preheat the oven to 350°F. Grease a 8½ x 4½ x 2½-inch loaf pan with shortening and dust with flour.

2 In a large mixing bowl, combine the applesauce, butter, and vanilla. In a separate medium mixing bowl, combine the 2 cups flour, the sugar, baking soda, allspice, cloves, cinnamon, and salt. Gradually add the dry ingredients to the wet ingredients, stirring until just incorporated. Stir in the chocolate chips. Pour the batter into the prepared pan. The pan should be about half full. Bake for 45 minutes, or until a toothpick inserted in the center comes out clean. Let cool completely before cutting and serving.

Crescent Roll
Casserole

Make this casserole when you're short on time but want something big on taste. It's a cinch to whip together, so even beginner cooks will earn oodles of praise. There are many variations of this type of casserole dish, but you'll find our personal favorite way of making this dish below. Want to be totally indulgent? Add another layer of crescent rolls to the top of the casserole. It's like your own bacon, egg, and cheese sandwich on a croissant roll! Indulgent? Yes. Tasty? You betcha!

✳ ✳ ✳ ✳ ✳

1 Preheat the oven to 350°F. Lightly coat a 9 x 13-inch baking dish with cooking spray.

2 Separate the crescent dough and press into the bottom and 1 inch up the sides of the prepared baking dish. Place the cheese slices over the dough.

3 In a small bowl, combine the eggs, milk, onion, and salt and pepper to taste. Pour the mixture over the cheese slices and sprinkle the casserole with the bacon. Cover loosely with tin foil, and bake for 1 hour or until the eggs are firm and the top is golden brown. Garnish with the chopped parsley and serve.

MAKES 6 TO 8 SERVINGS

Cooking spray

1 (8-ounce) can Pillsbury crescent rolls

6 to 7 thick slices Swiss cheese

4 large eggs

¾ cup whole milk

¼ cup finely chopped onion

Salt and freshly ground black pepper

6 slices bacon, cooked and crumbled

1 tablespoon chopped fresh parsley

Desserts Fit for a Queen

Blame it on our Southern roots, but we find the end of a meal is just another necessary excuse for a sweet indulgence. Gooey, rich chocolate, buttery pastry, fresh fruits, and other quality ingredients are essential to Casserole Queens desserts. From indulgent and decadent (try the Peanut Butter Freezer Pie with Chocolate and Bananas, page 182) to light and fluffy (Chu Chu's Tropical Trifle, page 188), these treats are easy to prepare and will win the hearts of even the most discriminating dessert aficionados! The Queens aren't afraid to love dessert, and they have gone the extra mile to bring you an array of cakes, pies, cobblers, and other goodies to delight your family and guests.

Gooey Apple Butter Cake

Chilled Coconut Cake

Yvette's Pineapple Upside-Down Cake

Bailey's Drug Store Chocolate Cake

Granny Haley's Orange Date Cake

Mom's Glazed Oatmeal Cake

Clementine Cake

Happily Sad Cake

Pollock's Peach Cobbler

Marge-Approved Caramel Bread Pudding

Peanut Butter Freezer Pie with Chocolate and Bananas

Not-So-Square Lemon Bars

Crunchy Peanut Butter Chocolate Bars

Blackberry Jiggle

Triple Chocolate Custard

Chu Chu's Tropical Trifle

Gooey Apple Butter Cake

MAKES 6 TO 8 SERVINGS

3 Granny Smith apples

1 tablespoon fresh lemon juice

1 (18.2-ounce) box yellow cake mix

1 cup (2 sticks) unsalted butter, melted

3 large eggs

1 (8-ounce) package cream cheese, softened

1½ teaspoons vanilla extract

1½ teaspoons ground cinnamon

3 cups confectioners' sugar

Crystal's nieces have nicknamed their mother "Butter." This term of endearment for Karen stems from the fact that she cooks everything with butter. One of her specialties is this cake, and—you guessed it—there's lots of butter! A cream cheese and apple mixture bakes up nice and gooey on top of a soft cake layer. Served warm, it just doesn't get any butter—we mean, better.

✳   ✳   ✳   ✳   ✳

1 Preheat the oven to 350°F.

2 Peel and slice the apples, then toss them in a bowl with the lemon juice to keep them from turning brown. Set aside.

3 In the bowl of a standing mixer fitted with the whisk attachment, add the cake mix, ½ cup of the melted butter, and one of the eggs. Mix for 2 minutes at medium-low speed. The batter should easily come together into a ball. Transfer the batter to a 9 x 13-inch baking dish and smooth the top with a spatula.

4 In the same bowl used for the batter, beat the cream cheese at medium-low speed for 30 seconds, until fluffy. Add the remaining ½ cup butter, the remaining 2 eggs, vanilla, and cinnamon. Beat on medium speed for 1 minute. Add the sugar and beat for 1 more minute.

5 Fold the apple slices into the cream cheese mixture, and spread the mixture over the cake mix in the baking dish.

6 Bake for 45 minutes or until the cake jiggles slightly when gently shaken and is somewhat solidified in the center. (The cream cheese mixture will not solidify completely.) Remove the cake from the oven and allow it to cool in the pan for 30 minutes.

7 Stored in the refrigerator, the cake will keep for three to four days, but it will never last that long!

 Great for freezing! See our Freezer Tips on pages 23–27.

Chilled Coconut Cake

MAKES 8 TO 10 SERVINGS

Vegetable shortening, such as Crisco

All-purpose flour

1 (18.2-ounce) box yellow cake mix

1 cup sugar

1 cup whole milk

1 (8-ounce) container frozen whipped topping, thawed

1 (7-ounce) bag sweetened coconut flakes

This cake is an everyday favorite at Crystal's mom's house. Any time Crystal's family gets together for a Sunday dinner, she has this tasty treat to look forward to. It got the nickname "Rice Cake" from Crystal's niece, Alexis, when she was little because she thought the coconut flakes were little pieces of rice.

1 Grease and flour a 9 x 13-inch metal casserole dish.

2 Follow the package instructions to mix the cake batter and bake the cake in the prepared casserole dish. While cake is still warm, poke holes in the top of it with a fork.

3 In a saucepan set over medium-low heat, combine the sugar and milk. Heat the mixture, stirring, until the sugar is dissolved; do not let boil. Pour the mixture over the cake, and let the cake cool completely.

4 Once the cake is cool, spread the whipped topping over the top of the cake. Cover the top of the cake with coconut flakes. Place the cake in the refrigerator and let it chill overnight.

5 Store any leftovers in the fridge for up to one week—the longer this cake is in the refrigerator, the better it gets!

Great for freezing! See our Freezer Tips on pages 23–27.

Yvette's Pineapple Upside-Down Cake

Yvette, Sandy's sister, is known all over the Valley for this cake. In fact, it's her claim to fame in those parts: "Oh, honey, you know Yvette. She's the one that makes that ridiculously tasty upside-down cake." Want in on her secret? She uses a cast-iron skillet to bake it, versus transferring it to a cake pan! This keeps the top of the cake extra crunchy and gives it a little extra caramelized flavor that people go crazy for.

MAKES 8 TO 10 SERVINGS

½ cup (1 stick) unsalted butter

1 cup packed light brown sugar

1 (20-ounce) can sliced pineapple in heavy syrup

1 (16-ounce) jar whole maraschino cherries

1 cup granulated sugar

3 large egg yolks

½ cup pineapple juice

3 large egg whites, lightly beaten

1 teaspoon baking powder

1 cup all-purpose flour

1 Preheat the oven to 325°F.

2 In a small saucepan set over medium heat, melt the butter. Add the brown sugar and cook until bubbly, about 10 minutes. Pour the caramel into a 9-inch cast-iron skillet. (Not to worry if you don't have a cast-iron skillet on-hand—you can use a metal 9 x 13-inch casserole dish instead.) Lay the pineapple slices evenly over the caramel, but don't overlap. Place a cherry in the center of each pineapple ring.

3 Beat together the granulated sugar and egg yolks until pale yellow. Add the pineapple juice, egg whites, baking powder, and flour. Pour the mixture over the pineapples. Bake for about 30 minutes or until a toothpick inserted into the center of the cake comes out clean. If the cake starts to brown too much, lay a piece of foil loosely over the cake while it finishes cooking.

4 Transfer the pan to a wire rack and let cool for 15 minutes. Invert the cake onto a serving platter. Serve while warm.

Bailey's Drug Store Chocolate Cake

MAKES 8 TO 10 SERVINGS

½ cup vegetable shortening, such as Crisco, plus more for greasing the dish

2 cups all-purpose flour, plus more for dusting the dish

2 cups sugar

2 large eggs

6 tablespoons unsweetened cocoa powder

2 teaspoons baking powder

1 teaspoon salt

1½ cups whole milk

1 teaspoon vanilla extract

Chocolate Frosting (recipe follows)

Bailey's Drug Store, in Blue Ridge, Georgia, is long gone, but the cake lives on. Crystal's Aunt Mary Ann and Aunt Thelma used to love eating this cake with ice cream during their lunch break at work. Both were hardworking women in the '50s and they needed this daily treat to keep them going. Every now and then, couldn't you also use a little noontime sweet to get you through the day? Don't cheat yourself. It is better with ice cream, so make sure and give yourself a big scoop! We suggest good ol' vanilla!

1 Preheat the oven to 350°F. Grease and flour a 9 x 13-inch casserole dish.

2 Using a whisk, beat together the sugar and ½ cup shortening. Add the eggs, and whisk until light in color. Add the 2 cups flour and stir until combined.

3 In a separate bowl, combine the cocoa powder, baking powder, and salt. Add the dry ingredients to the sugar mixture alternately with the milk, stirring to combine after each addition. Add the vanilla and stir until combined.

4 Pour the batter into the prepared casserole dish. Bake for 45 minutes or until a toothpick inserted in the center comes out clean. Transfer the baking dish to a wire rack and let the cake cool completely.

5 Spread the chocolate frosting over the top of the cake. The cake will keep in the refrigerator, wrapped in plastic wrap, for five days.

Chocolate Frosting

1 In a saucepan set over medium-high heat, combine the butter, sugar, salt, vanilla, cocoa powder, and evaporated milk. Bring to a boil and cook, stirring constantly, for 4 minutes.

2 Transfer the frosting to the bowl of a standing mixer fitted with the whisk attachment, and beat for 1 to 2 minutes, or until it is thick enough to spread.

3 The frosting can be made ahead and stored in an airtight container in the refrigerator for up to five days.

MAKES ABOUT 2½ CUPS

½ cup (1 stick) unsalted butter

2 cups sugar

¼ teaspoon salt

2 teaspoons vanilla extract

¼ cup unsweetened cocoa powder

1 (5-ounce) can evaporated milk

Granny Haley's Orange Date Cake

MAKES 8 TO 10 SERVINGS

Vegetable shortening, such as Crisco

2 cups all-purpose flour, plus more for dusting the dish

1 cup chopped dates

¼ cup (½ stick) unsalted butter

1 cup granulated sugar

2 large eggs

½ teaspoon baking powder

½ teaspoon baking soda

⅔ cups sour milk (see headnote)

2 tablespoons grated orange zest

½ cup chopped pecans

1 cup confectioners' sugar

2 tablespoons orange juice

This recipe was a favorite of Sandy's Granny Haley. Sandy remembers how Granny Haley would serve this cake whenever anyone would come by for a Sunday afternoon visit over coffee or tea. The subtly sweet cake was the perfect snack and accompaniment to their ever sweeter conversation.

Most people don't have sour milk on hand, so here's a simple way to make some. Combine ⅔ cup milk and ⅔ teaspoon white vinegar or lemon juice, and let it sit for 10 minutes before using.

1 Preheat the oven to 350°F. Grease and flour a 9 x 13-inch casserole dish.

2 Put the dates in a bowl and cover them with hot water. Let them soak for 1 hour.

3 In a separate bowl, cream together the butter, granulated sugar, and eggs.

4 Sift the 2 cups flour, the baking powder, and baking soda into a medium bowl. Add the dry ingredients to the butter and sugar mixture alternately with milk, adding a third of each at a time and mixing thoroughly before adding the next. Drain the dates and stir them in with the orange zest and nuts. Pour the batter into the prepared casserole dish. Bake for 40 to 50 minutes or until a toothpick when inserted into the center of the cake comes out clean.

5 Meanwhile, whisk together the confectioners' sugar and orange juice, making sure to break up any lumps. The consistency should be such that it can be easily drizzled or

poured over the cake. If it's too thick, thin it with a little more orange juice; if it's too thin, add more confectioners' sugar, a teaspoon at a time, making sure to mix thoroughly before adding more. Drizzle the orange glaze over the cake while it is still warm. Cut into squares and serve while warm.

6 Store leftover pieces in an airtight container at room temperature for up to five days.

There were many funny stories that came out of these visits at Granny Haley's, but this one takes the cake— literally! Sandy's Uncle Dale and his friend Kiefer were cooks in the army. One day, they discovered that their kitchen was being raided every night by hungry soldiers with a sweet tooth. To teach the thieves a lesson, Kiefer made a special cake full of shrimp shells. But in an unexpected turn of events, some high-ranked officers stopped by for a special meeting and the cakes meant for the thieves got served to the VIPs. Kiefer and Dale just knew they were going to be discharged, but not one word was ever mentioned. Maybe the officers were simply used to eating bad mess-hall food.

Mom's Glazed Oatmeal Cake

MAKES 8 TO 10 SERVINGS

½ cup vegetable shortening, such as Crisco, plus more for greasing the dish

1⅓ cups all-purpose flour, plus more for dusting the dish

1¼ cups hot water

1 cup old-fashioned rolled oats

1¾ cups packed light brown sugar

1 cup granulated sugar

2 large eggs

1 teaspoon baking soda

1 teaspoon ground cinnamon

½ teaspoon salt

6 tablespoons (¾ stick) unsalted butter

1 tablespoon evaporated milk

1 cup chopped pecans

1 cup sweetened coconut flakes

Both Sandy and Crystal's love for cooking stems from their mothers. This particular recipe is one that Sandy and her mother, Marge, shared throughout her youth, and it signifies that mother-daughter bond. What better place to get to know your kids than through cooking your favorite recipes in the kitchen?

1 Preheat the oven to 350°F. Lightly grease and flour a 9 x 13-inch casserole dish.

2 In a small bowl, pour the hot water over the oats and let sit for 10 minutes for the oats to absorb the water.

3 Cream together 1 cup of the brown sugar, granulated sugar, and ½ cup of the shortening in a large bowl. Add the eggs and stir well.

4 In a separate bowl, sift together the 1⅓ cups flour, baking soda, cinnamon, and salt. Add the dry ingredients to the butter mixture, and stir well. Add the softened oats a little at a time, stirring after each addition, until all of the oats are incorporated.

5 Pour the batter into the prepared casserole dish. Bake for 30 minutes or until a toothpick inserted into the center of the cake comes out clean. Transfer the cake to a wire rack and let cool completely.

6 Preheat the broiler.

7 For the icing, put the remaining ¾ cup brown sugar, the butter, evaporated milk, and nuts in a saucepan set over medium-high heat and bring to a boil. Boil for 1 minute. Remove the pan from the heat and add the coconut.

8 Ice the cake, transfer it to the oven, and broil for 3 to 5 minutes or until the icing is golden brown. Watch the cake very carefully as the icing can burn easily. Cut into square pieces and serve immediately.

9 Store any leftover pieces in an airtight container and refrigerate for up to five days.

Clementine Cake

MAKES 8 TO 10 SERVINGS

Vegetable shortening, such as Crisco

All-purpose flour

¾ cup water

1 (18.2-ounce) box white cake mix

4 large egg whites, lightly beaten

½ cup plus 5 to 6 teaspoons clementine juice (from about 7 clementines)

¼ cup canola oil

1½ teaspoons grated clementine zest

4 clementines, peeled, sectioned, and membranes removed

⅓ cup unsalted butter, softened

3 cups confectioners' sugar

¾ cup semi-sweet chocolate chips, for garnish

24 clementine sections with membranes removed (about 2½ clementines), for garnish

"Oh, my darling, oh, my darling"—you'll be singing this sweet, sweet song until you bite into this, one of our favorite cakes. Then you'll forget all about singing and focus your attention on the delicious citrus flavor mixed ever so delicately in a moist white cake. A cross between sweet oranges and Chinese mandarins, clementines add a touch of unexpected sweetness—and are what make the cake, in our opinion. Pun intended.

✳   ✳   ✳   ✳   ✳

1 Preheat the oven to 350°F. Grease and flour a 9½ x 13-inch casserole dish.

2 In the bowl of a electric mixer fitted with the whisk attachment, combine the water, cake mix, egg whites, ½ cup of the clementine juice, the canola oil, and 1 teaspoon of the clementine zest. Beat on low speed for 30 seconds. Increase the speed to medium and beat for 2 minutes. Pour the batter into the prepared casserole dish. Place the sections from 2 clementines evenly across the top of the batter; gently press down into batter. Chop the remaining 2 clementines' sections and sprinkle over the batter. Bake for 15 to 20 minutes or until a toothpick inserted in the center comes out clean. Cool for 10 minutes, then remove the cake from the pan and set it on a wire rack to cool completely.

3 To make the frosting, in a small bowl, beat the butter until light and fluffy. Add the confectioners' sugar, remaining ½ teaspoon clementine zest, and 5 teaspoons of clementine juice, and beat with a wire whisk until combined. If the frosting is too thick to spread, thin it by adding more juice. Frost the cooled cake.

4 In a small microwave-safe bowl, melt the chocolate chips and stir until smooth. Dip the clementine sections for the garnish halfway into the chocolate and allow the excess to drip off. Place on a waxed paper–lined baking sheet; refrigerate until set.

5 To serve, cut the cake into slices and place one chocolate-dipped clementine section on each slice.

Happily Sad Cake

MAKES 8 TO 10 SERVINGS

Vegetable shortening, such as Crisco

All-purpose flour

2 cups Bisquick biscuit mix

1 pound packed dark brown sugar

3 large eggs

1 tablespoon vanilla extract

¼ teaspoon salt

¾ cup chopped pecans or walnuts

Pecan praline ice cream, for serving

This recipe is courtesy of our sweet friend Julie, whose cousin gave it this name because the cake does not actually rise. The final product comes out flat and dense, so it is kind of a sad-looking cake, but once you taste how chewy and delicious it is, brownies will take a back-row seat to this low riser.

1 Preheat the oven to 350°F. Grease and flour a 9 x 13-inch baking dish. Set aside.

2 In a large bowl, combine the Bisquick, brown sugar, eggs, vanilla, and salt. Add the pecans and stir well. Pour the batter into the prepared baking dish. Bake for 30 to 35 minutes or until a toothpick inserted into the center of the cake comes out clean. Let the cake cool in the pan for 30 minutes. Cut into squares and serve it with pecan praline ice cream!

3 Store leftovers in an airtight container in the refrigerator for up to five days.

Pollock's Peach Cobbler

Always a hit! Sandy's version of peach cobbler starts with a layer of cakelike pastry: moist and delicious—never dry! It's spiced with nutmeg and cinnamon to accentuate the warm flavor of the peaches and simply can't be beat when accompanied by a scoop of ice cream. We recommend trying cinnamon ice cream for the ultimate flavor combination!

1 Preheat the oven to 350°F. Pour the melted butter into a 9 x 13-inch casserole dish and set aside.

2 In a large bowl, combine 1 cup of the sugar, the flour, baking powder, and salt. Stir in the milk and egg. Pour the mixture evenly over melted butter in the pan.

3 In a separate medium bowl, combine the remaining 1 cup sugar, the peaches, cinnamon, and nutmeg. Spread the peaches over the batter. Bake for 35 to 45 minutes, until the crust is golden brown and the edges are bubbling.

4 Let the cobbler cool for 5 minutes before dusting lightly with confectioners' sugar.

Great for freezing! See our Freezer Tips on pages 23–27.

MAKES 6 TO 8 SERVINGS

½ cup (1 stick) unsalted butter, melted

2 cups sugar

1 cup all-purpose flour

2 teaspoons baking powder

¼ teaspoon salt

⅔ cup whole milk, at room temperature

1 large egg, at room temperature

1 (28-ounce) can sliced peaches, drained

2 teaspoons ground cinnamon

½ teaspoon ground nutmeg

Confectioners' sugar

Marge-Approved Caramel Bread Pudding

MAKES 8 SERVINGS

8 large eggs

3 cups sugar

2 cups whole milk

2 cups heavy cream

¼ cup brandy

¼ teaspoon salt

1 vanilla bean

1 baguette, cut into 1-inch pieces

½ teaspoon white vinegar

3 tablespoons unsalted butter

Sandy's mom, Margie (aka Marge), has a passion for bread pudding and is a self-proclaimed connoisseur. This is the only bread pudding out of a pile of test recipes that Marge gave her stamp of approval, noting it was the richness of the vanilla custard that won her over. Go ahead and try it. Marge approves!

✳ ✳ ✳ ✳ ✳

1 In a large bowl, whisk the eggs. Add 2 cups of the sugar, the milk, cream, brandy, and salt. Split the vanilla bean lengthwise, scrape the seeds into the bowl, and whisk well. Add bread, then place bowl in the refrigerator and let soak for 45 minutes to 1 hour, pushing bread down occasionally to submerge it, until most of the liquid has been absorbed.

2 Meanwhile, in a medium saucepan set over high heat, combine the remaining 1 cup sugar, the vinegar, and ½ cup water and stir until the sugar has dissolved. Cook, without stirring, until the sugar is dark amber in color, 7 to 10 minutes. Remove the pan from the heat and carefully add ¼ cup water (mixture will spatter). Swirl the pot until combined.

3 Working quickly, pour the very hot caramel into a 9 x 13-inch metal casserole dish (a glass pan can crack with extreme high temperatures), carefully rotating the pan so that the caramel covers the bottom and some of the sides; let set aside until cool.

4 Preheat the oven to 350°F. Put a kettle of water on to boil.

5 Rub the cooled caramel sauce and the sides of casserole dish with the butter, and spoon in the bread mixture, packing tightly to fit. Cover the top of the bread with parchment paper.

6 Place the casserole dish in a large roasting pan and pour hot water into the roasting pan until it comes halfway up the sides of the dish. Bake the pudding 1¼ hours or until a knife inserted into the center comes out barely clean. Do not overbake. Let stand for 5 minutes. Serve warm.

7 Store leftovers in an airtight container in the refrigerator for up to five days.

Peanut Butter Freezer Pie
with Chocolate and Bananas

MAKES 8 TO 10 SERVINGS

Cooking spray

1½ cups vanilla wafer cookies (about 30 cookies)

1½ cups packed light brown sugar

3 tablespoons unsalted butter, melted

4 ounces cream cheese, softened

½ cup creamy peanut butter

½ teaspoon vanilla extract

2 (8-ounce) containers frozen whipped topping, thawed

2 cups sliced banana (about 2 bananas)

½ cup chocolate syrup

It's bananas how good this dessert is! Seriously, it doesn't get much better than this. A creamy peanut butter topping covers layers of fresh bananas and a tasty vanilla-wafer crust. Drizzled with a rich chocolate sauce, we think it's the best in the bunch!

1 Coat a 9 x 13-inch casserole dish with cooking spray.

2 Pulse the cookies in a food processor until finely ground. Add ½ cup of the brown sugar and the butter; pulse two to three times or just until combined. Press the crumb mixture into the bottom of the prepared casserole dish. Set aside.

3 Put the remaining 1 cup brown sugar, the cream cheese, peanut butter, and vanilla in the bowl of a standing mixer fitted with a whisk attachment. Beat at medium speed until smooth. Fold in the whipped topping.

4 Lay the banana slices on the prepared crust and drizzle with the chocolate syrup. Spread the peanut butter mixture over the bananas and drizzle again with the chocolate syrup. Cover with plastic wrap and freeze until frozen through, about 5 hours. Let stand at room temperature for about 10 minutes before serving.

5 To store, cover with plastic wrap and refrigerate for up to two days.

Not-So-Square Lemon Bars

Tart and tangy, lemon bars are one of those amazing desserts that seem to please everyone. Maybe it's because bars are easy to serve and highly portable, a clever cross between a cookie and pie.

The key to a good lemon bar is a strong citrus flavor. You'll want your mouth to pucker in delight! When choosing your lemons, be sure to pick ones that are vibrant in color and feel somewhat heavy in the hand. Also, when zesting, be sure you only get the yellow part, as the white part is very bitter.

1 Preheat the oven to 350°F.

2 Mix 2 cups of the flour, the butter, confectioners' sugar, and salt in a bowl. Press the mixture into the bottom of a 9 x 13-inch baking dish. Bake for 20 minutes or until golden brown. Transfer to a wire rack to cool. Keep oven at 350°F.

3 In the bowl of an electric mixer fitted with the whisk attachment, beat the eggs and granulated sugar until smooth. Add the remaining 6 tablespoons of flour, the lemon juice, and lemon zest and beat until well combined. Pour the filling over the prepared crust, and bake for 25 minutes or until filling has set. Transfer the baking dish to a wire rack and let cool completely. Sprinkle with confectioners' sugar before cutting into bars.

4 Store leftovers in an airtight container in the refrigerator for up to five days.

MAKES 10 TO 12 SERVINGS

2 cups plus 6 tablespoons all-purpose flour

1 cup (2 sticks) unsalted butter, softened

½ cup sifted confectioners' sugar, plus more for sprinkling

Pinch of salt

4 large eggs

2 cups granulated sugar

6 tablespoons fresh lemon juice

1 tablespoon lemon zest

When life gives you lemons, remember Crystal's rule of thumb: 1 medium lemon yields 2 to 4 tablespoons of juice and 1 tablespoon of grated rind.

Crunchy Peanut Butter Chocolate Bars

MAKE 12 SERVINGS

1 cup (2 sticks) unsalted butter

6 cups mini marshmallows

6 cups Rice Krispies cereal

Cooking spray

1¾ cups confectioners' sugar

1 cup creamy peanut butter

¾ cup graham cracker crumbs

⅔ cup evaporated milk

1⅔ cups granulated sugar

½ teaspoon salt

1½ cups bittersweet chocolate chips

1 teaspoon vanilla extract

Rice Krispies? Check. Peanut Butter? Check. Chocolate? Check. Delicious on their own, these three flavors will knock your socks off when layered together. The bars are decadent and rich, so be sure to have a glass of milk handy.

✳ ✳ ✳ ✳ ✳

1 In a large saucepan set over low heat, melt 4 tablespoons of the butter. Add 4 cups of the marshmallows and stir until melted. Remove the pan from the heat and add the cereal. Stir until the cereal is coated. Press the mixture into the bottom of a greased 9 x 13-inch casserole dish. Coat your hands with butter and press the mixture into the pan. Using a chopstick, poke many holes in the layer. Set the pan aside.

2 In a medium saucepan set over low heat, melt ½ cup of the butter. Remove the pan from the heat and stir in the confectioners' sugar. Add the peanut butter and graham cracker crumbs, stirring until well combined. Spread the mixture evenly over the Rice Krispies layer. Using a chopstick, poke many holes in the layer. Let cool completely.

3 In a medium saucepan set over medium heat, combine the remaining 4 tablespoons butter, the evaporated milk, granulated sugar, and salt and bring to a boil; cook 4 to 5 minutes, stirring constantly. Remove from the heat. Stir in the remaining 2 cups marshmallows, the chocolate, and vanilla. Beat for 1 minute until the marshmallows are melted. Pour over the peanut butter fudge, spread evenly, and place in the refrigerator to harden, about 2 hours.

4 To serve, cut into 1-inch squares. Store in an airtight container at room temperature for up to five days.

Blackberry Jiggle

Jell-O has gotten a bad rap, and we are not sure why. In fact, Jell-O happens to be one of the Queens' favorite go-to treats, as it's now available in low-calorie and sugar-free varieties, making it a wonderful vehicle for satisfying your sweet tooth without all the guilt. And, Jell-O is extremely versatile. With dozens of flavors available to choose from, you can always find a satisfying one. If you haven't had Jell-O in a while, we invite you to try this recipe. It's the perfect, cool treat for the summertime that's both light and fruity. Besides, desserts that jiggle are fun!

MAKES 10 SERVINGS

4 cups boiling water

2 (6-ounce) packages blackberry-flavored Jell-O

2 (15-ounce) cans blueberries, or 2 cups frozen blueberries, thawed

1 (20-ounce) can crushed pineapple

2 (8-ounce) packages cream cheese

2 cups sugar

2 pints sour cream

2 teaspoons vanilla extract

1½ cups chopped pecans

1　Combine the boiling water and Jell-O in a large bowl, stirring until the Jell-O is dissolved.

2　Drain the liquid from the blueberries and pineapple into a measuring cup. Add enough water to make 4 cups and add to the Jell-O.

3　Put the mixture in the refrigerator and chill for 1 hour.

4　Stir the blueberries and pineapple into the Jell-O. Pour the mixture into 9 x 13-inch casserole dish. Cover, transfer to the refrigerator, and chill until firm.

5　Combine the cream cheese, sugar, sour cream, and vanilla in a medium bowl. Spread over the top of the chilled Jell-O, then sprinkle with the nuts. Return to the refrigerator and chill for 1 hour or until set. Cut into squares and serve cold.

Triple Chocolate Custard

MAKES 8 TO 10 SERVINGS

Cooking spray

1 (16.6-ounce) bag Oreo cookies

¾ cup (1½ sticks) unsalted butter, melted

4 ounces bittersweet chocolate chips

4 ounces milk chocolate chips

4 ounces white chocolate chips

¼ cup water

1 tablespoon unflavored gelatin

5 large egg yolks

¼ cup sugar

1 cup half-and-half

1¾ cups chilled whipping cream

Calling all chocolate lovers! No matter what kind of chocolate you like, this dish is for you. Decadent layers of dark, milk, and white chocolate on an Oreo cookie base—you can close your mouth now.

1 Coat a 9 x 13-inch casserole dish with cooking spray and set aside.

2 Pulse the Oreo cookies in a food processor until roughly ground. Slowly add the butter and pulse until the Oreo crumbs just start to hold together. Pour the mixture into the prepared pan and press into the bottom.

3 Put each of the types of chocolate chips in separate medium bowls.

4 Combine the water and gelatin in a small bowl. Let stand for 10 minutes or until the gelatin softens.

5 Meanwhile, in the bowl of an electric mixer fitted with the whisk attachment, beat the egg yolks and sugar for 5 minutes or until the mixture is pale yellow and very thick. Bring the half-and-half just to a simmer in a large, heavy saucepan set over medium-high heat. Gradually whisk the hot half-and-half into the eggs, then pour the egg mixture into the saucepan. Stir over medium heat until the custard thickens and coats the back of a spoon, about 3 minutes (do not boil). Remove the custard from the heat. Add the softened gelatin, and stir until the gelatin dissolves.

6 Strain the gelatin mixture into large glass measuring cup. Immediately pour one-third of the hot custard into each

bowl of chocolate chips. Stir each chocolate with a separate spoon until melted and smooth. (If the mixture cools before the chocolate is completely melted, set the bowl over a saucepan of simmering water and stir just until the chocolate melts.) Let the chocolate mixtures cool to room temperature, stirring occasionally, about 30 minutes.

7 In the bowl of an electric mixer fitted with the whisk attachment, beat the cream until stiff peaks form. Divide the whipped cream equally among the bowls of chocolate, using about 1⅓ cups of whipped cream for each. Fold the whipped cream into the chocolates in each bowl with a rubber spatula.

8 Pour the bittersweet chocolate mixture into bottom of the prepared pan. Smooth the top with a spatula, then chill for 10 minutes. Spread the milk chocolate mixture over the bittersweet chocolate layer. Smooth the top with a spatula, then chill for 10 minutes. Spread the white chocolate mixture over the milk chocolate layer. Smooth the top with a spatula, and chill until firm, about 1 hour.

9 To store, cover the pan tightly with plastic wrap and refrigerate for up to four days.

Chu Chu's Tropical Trifle

MAKES 8 TO 10 SERVINGS

2 cups whole milk

6 large egg yolks

1½ cups sugar

⅓ cup cornstarch

¼ cup (½ stick) unsalted butter, cut into small pieces

½ cup sweetened coconut flakes

1 cup water

1 teaspoon corn syrup

Seeds scraped from 1 vanilla bean

1 cup fresh pineapple chunks (½ inch)

1 teaspoon dark rum

1 (3-ounce) store-bought ladyfingers

¼ cup whipped cream

1 cup unsweetened coconut flakes

We know that we wouldn't be where we are today without the continued support and encouragement we receive from our customers. To thank them, we held a recipe contest for which the winner's dish would be featured in our book. Cristiane Diehl (aka Chu Chu), that's you! Take a bow. You deserve it. Your trifle is out of this world! (Well, at least out of this country—it's from Brazil!)

* * * * *

1 Preheat the oven to 350°F.

2 Bring the milk to a boil in a small saucepan set over medium-high heat, stirring constantly to prevent the milk from scalding.

3 In a medium saucepan (no heat), whisk the egg yolks, ½ cup of the sugar, and the cornstarch until the mixture is thick and well blended. While whisking constantly, drizzle in about ¼ cup of the hot milk (this will temper, or warm, the yolks so they won't curdle). Continue whisking and slowly pour in the rest of the milk. Set the pan over medium heat. While whisking vigorously, bring the mixture to a boil, and cook, whisking constantly, for 1 to 2 minutes or until very thick. Remove the pan from the heat. Let the mixture cool for 5 minutes. Whisk in the butter piece by piece, whisking until fully incorporated and the cream is smooth and silky.

4 Meanwhile, toast the coconut. Spread it out on a sheet pan in an even layer, then place in the oven and bake for about 20 minutes, stirring every 5 minutes to make sure it browns evenly, until it's golden (see Note). Fold the toasted coconut into the egg mixture. Transfer to a bowl and press a piece of plastic wrap against the surface of the coconut

cream to create an airtight seal. Refrigerate until cold, about 2 hours.

5 In a medium saucepan set over medium-high heat, combine the water, remaining 1 cup sugar, the corn syrup, and vanilla seeds. Bring the mixture to a boil. Cook until the sugar is dissolved, after about 2 minutes, then add the pineapple chunks and rum. Reduce the heat to medium and cook until the pineapple is translucent, about 10 minutes. Remove the pan from the heat and set aside to cool. Strain the syrup from the pineapple compote into a shallow dish. Set the compote aside.

6 Dip the ladyfingers one by one into the pineapple syrup and place them in the bottom of a 9 x 13-inch casserole dish. Spread two-thirds of the coconut cream on top of the ladyfingers. Spread the pineapple compote on top of the coconut cream.

7 Whisk together the whipped cream and the remaining coconut cream. Spread the mixture on top of the trifle and scatter the coconut flakes over the top to finish. Refrigerate for 3 hours to allow the flavors to blend. Serve cold.

Toasting coconut is not hard, but you have to watch closely, as the coconut can go from almost done to burnt in what feels like a matter of seconds. To save time (and for less stress), try toasting the coconut in the microwave. Spread the coconut evenly on a microwave-safe plate. Microwave on high at 30-second intervals and toss until lightly browned.

From Scratch.
Yes, You Can.

So you love cooking and want to take a little more time to make something extra special? Add a little more love? We understand completely. It's all a part of *sophistakitch*—that extra gourmet flair that people will notice. In this chapter, you'll find a number of recipes that will help you create our dishes entirely from scratch. Such as preparing your own soups and broths to give your dish that flavor you crave, without additives or preservatives. And fresh bread crumbs are always tastier than packaged, not to mention an economical way to use leftover bread! We understand that you are pursuing the pinnacle of taste, and we're here to help. When you're done, don't forget to pat yourself on the back. You've just put some extra lovin' in your oven.

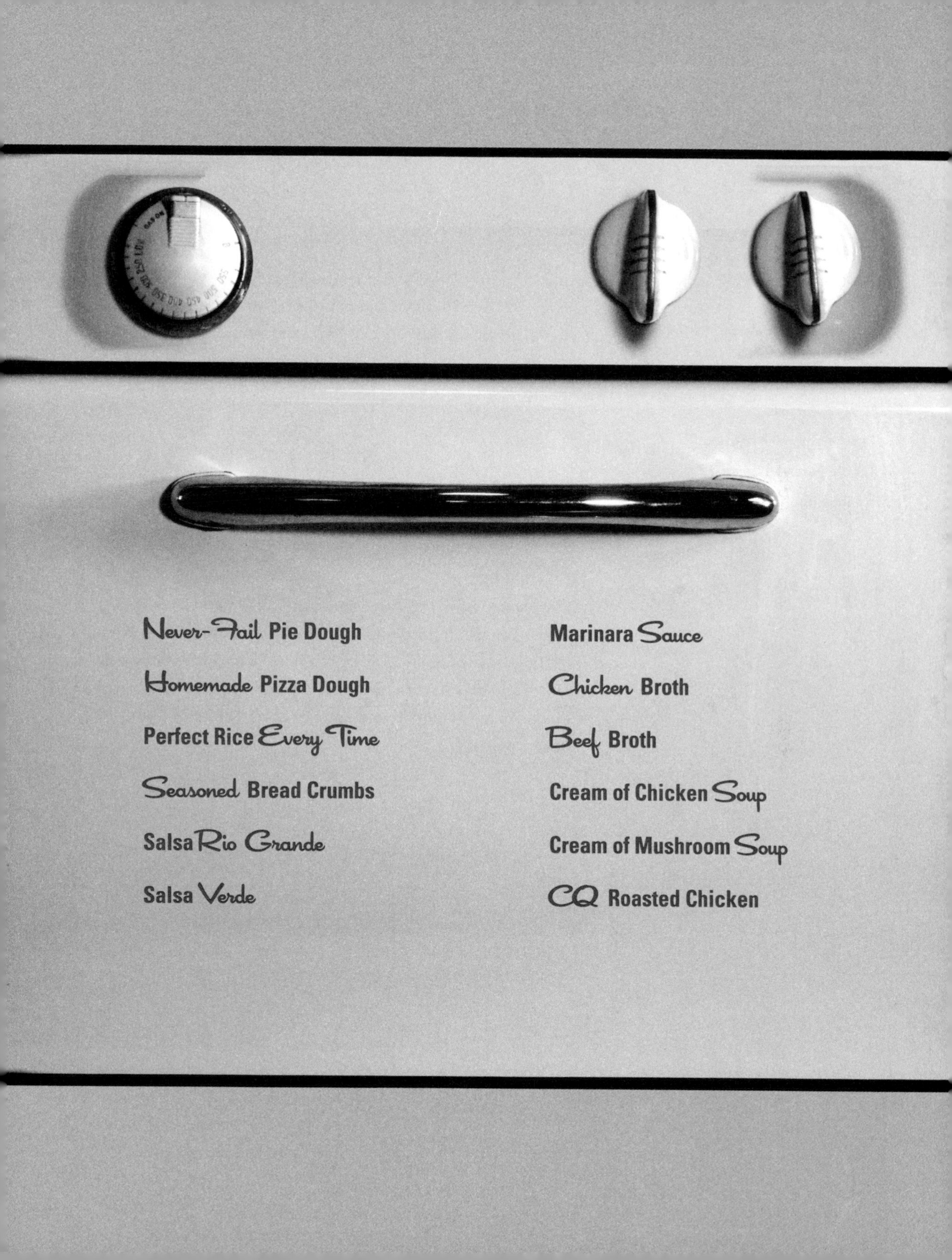

Never-Fail Pie Dough

Homemade Pizza Dough

Perfect Rice Every Time

Seasoned Bread Crumbs

Salsa Rio Grande

Salsa Verde

Marinara Sauce

Chicken Broth

Beef Broth

Cream of Chicken Soup

Cream of Mushroom Soup

CQ Roasted Chicken

Never-Fail Pie Dough

MAKES TWO 9-INCH PIE CRUSTS

1¼ cups vegetable shortening, such as Crisco

3 cups all-purpose flour

1 teaspoon salt

1 large egg, well beaten

1 tablespoon white vinegar

5 tablespoons ice water

Ding! Clever recipe alert for a reliable pie crust you'll make again and again! Double ding! Cute gift alert! Next time you're making your favorite pie, double the recipe and whip up some adorable individual-sized pies using half-pint glass jars (see recipe on opposite page). For ease of use, purchase the widest-mouth jar you can find.

1 With a pastry cutter or two forks, cut the shortening into the flour and salt in a large bowl, or place in a food processor and pulse until the texture is like sand.

2 In a small bowl, combine the egg, vinegar, and ice water. Pour the wet ingredients into the flour mixture all at once. Stir with a spoon until all of the flour is moistened, or pulse in a food processor until the dough comes together in a ball. Wrap the dough in plastic wrap and chill for 1 hour before using.

If you don't plan to use your dough immediately, you can freeze the dough with great results! Form a ½-inch-thick dough disk, then wrap in plastic wrap and place in freezer until firm, about 2 hours. Once firm, place the dough disk in a freezer bag. Dough will last for up to two months in the freezer.

Mini Pies

MAKES ENOUGH FOR 6 MINI PIES

Prepare the dough according to the recipe. On a floured surface, roll it out into a ⅛-inch-thick circle. Use the ring of a jar to cut out perfectly sized pie tops. Cut at least one hole in each top to keep the pies from bursting when cooking. Use the rest of the dough to line the jars—no need to grease!—by taking little pieces and pressing them on the bottom and up the sides of the jars. Fill each with a ½ cup of your favorite pie filling and add a pie crust top, sealing the edges tightly. Place the lids on the jars and store the mini pies in your freezer.

If presenting the pies as a gift, remove the outer band of the lid, place a square of decorative fabric over the inner lid of the jar, then screw the outer band back on tightly. Add personalized labels with these instructions for cooking: No need to thaw. Simply remove lids and place jars on a sheet pan in a cold oven. Cook at 350°F for 50 to 60 minutes or until the pie crust is golden brown.

Homemade Pizza Dough

MAKES ONE 9 X 13-INCH CRUST

½ teaspoon sugar

1 cup warm water (110° to 115°F)

1 package active dry yeast (2½ teaspoons)

2½ cups all-purpose flour

½ cup yellow cornmeal

¾ teaspoon salt

2 tablespoons olive oil, plus more for the bowl

Nothing is better than pizza dough made from scratch. For the pizza connoisseur (and the pizza consumer), the crust can make or break the whole pie. It does take some extra time and patience, but we promise that it is well worth the effort.

1 In a large bowl, dissolve the sugar in the warm water. Sprinkle the yeast over the water and let stand until foamy, about 5 minutes. Stir in 2¼ cups of the flour, the cornmeal, salt, and 2 tablespoons of the oil, stirring until the mixture forms a dough. Put the dough on a floured surface and knead, incorporating as much of the remaining ¼ cup flour as necessary to prevent the dough from sticking, until smooth and elastic, about 5 minutes.

2 Put the dough in a deep, oiled bowl and turn to coat with the oil. Cover the bowl with plastic wrap and let the dough rise in a warm place for 1 hour or until doubled in bulk.

 If you don't plan to use the pizza dough within two days of making it, form the dough into a disk and place in a zip-top freezer bag. The dough will last in the freezer for up to two months.

 Pizza Dough is not just for pizza anymore! It is a very flexible building block for tasty treats. Sandy likes to roll it out, brush it with melted butter, and sprinkle with cinnamon sugar for a quick and sweet dessert.

Perfect Rice *Every Time*

For even the most seasoned chefs, rice can prove to be a challenge. Yes, rice. One minute short and it's soggy; a minute extra, it can be sticky and clumped together. Unless you want to spend your hard-earned money on a rice steamer, we suggest you follow this tried-and-true method.

MAKES 3 CUPS

1 cup long-grain rice

1 teaspoon salt

1 Put the rice and salt in a 2-quart saucepan, add 2 cups of water, and cover the pan with a tight-fitting lid. Bring to a boil, then reduce the heat to the lowest possible setting. Cook for 14 minutes.

2 Turn off heat and let the rice steam in the pan for 5 more minutes. Fluff the rice with a fork.

Seasoned Bread Crumbs

MAKES 3 CUPS

1 loaf day-old bread

2 tablespoons dried thyme or oregano

2 tablespoons dried basil or parsley

1 teaspoon garlic powder

2 teaspoons salt

½ teaspoon freshly ground black pepper

Bread is too good of a thing to let go to waste. How many times does your uneaten bread go to the birds? If for some insane reason you didn't eat the entire baguette for dinner, use the leftovers to make some delicious bread crumbs, which are always handy for adding texture to casseroles. Bread crumbs can go stale quickly, so keep them fresh longer by storing in the freezer.

1 Preheat the oven to 300°F.

2 Cut the bread into 1-inch cubes and pulse in a food processor to make coarse crumbs. Spread the crumbs on a baking sheet and dry them out by baking for 10 to 15 minutes, stirring after 5 minutes. Allow the crumbs to cool completely.

3 Return the dried crumbs to the food processor. Add the thyme, basil, garlic powder, salt, and pepper, then pulse until the crumbs are finely processed and well mixed with the seasoning.

4 Store in an airtight container for up to six months.

Salsa
Rio Grande

Salsa is Sandy's condiment of choice. (Well, that and pickled jalapeños!) This recipe is one of her absolute favorites and provides her with a little taste of home. She typically adds this salsa to her morning eggs (she's spicy that way) or serves it as a flavorful dip to sit alongside a big pile of tortilla chips. If you like a really hot salsa, leave in some of the jalapeño seeds.

MAKES 2 CUPS

1 large onion, finely chopped

3 garlic cloves, minced

1 jalapeño pepper, cored, seeds removed, and finely chopped

4 medium tomatoes, chopped

½ teaspoon ground cumin

¼ cup chopped fresh cilantro

1 tablespoon fresh lime juice

Salt and freshly ground black pepper

2 to 3 dashes of hot sauce

1 In a medium bowl, combine the onion, garlic, jalapeños, tomatoes, cumin, cilantro, lime juice, salt, pepper, and hot sauce.

2 The salsa can be stored in an airtight container in the refrigerator for up to two weeks.

Salsa Verde

MAKES 2 CUPS

8 tomatillos, husked and washed (see Note)

1 medium onion, roughly chopped

1 jalapeño pepper, cored, seeds removed, and chopped

3 garlic cloves, roughly chopped

½ cup chopped fresh cilantro

1½ tablespoons fresh lime juice

Salt and freshly ground black pepper

This zesty salsa gets its flavor and green hue from tomatillos. Tomatillos have a tart, citrus-like flavor that works as a zingy accompaniment to fish (see Halibut Enchiladas with Salsa Verde, page 86). When choosing tomatillos, smaller is better. The smaller ones have a sweeter taste. Tomatillos should be green and about the size of a large cherry tomato. The inside is white and meatier than a tomato. They are covered by a papery husk that may range from the pale green to a light brown. The husks are inedible and should be removed before use.

1 Into a pot of boiling water put the tomatillos, onion, jalapeño, and garlic, and cook for about 8 minutes. Strain the vegetables from the pot and reserve the cooking liquid.

2 Put the vegetables and cilantro in a blender or food processor and pulse. Add the reserved cooking liquid ½ cup at a time and process to the consistency of a pourable puree.

3 Transfer to a large bowl, add the lime juice, and season with salt and pepper to taste.

4 The sauce can be stored in an airtight container in the refrigerator for up to two weeks.

If you can't find fresh tomatillos in your local supermarket, you can use a 28-ounce can of tomatillos. The flavor of the canned isn't as bright as the fresh, but it's not too shabby in a pinch!

Marinara Sauce

Fuggedaboutit! Marinara sauce is a great thing to have on hand at all times to make a fast and flavorful meal. Double or triple this recipe and freeze the sauce in pint-sized containers. Just pull out of your freezer and make a quick and delicious dinner by tossing it with cooked pasta. Or for a quick snack, spoon on some toasted Italian bread and sprinkle with your favorite cheese (Parmesan and mozzarella work nicely).

✳ ✳ ✳ ✳ ✳

1 Heat the olive oil in a medium saucepan set over medium heat. Add the garlic and shallots, and sauté until the garlic starts to brown, about 5 minutes. Do not burn the garlic or your sauce will be bitter. Add the tomatoes with their juice, basil, red pepper flakes, oregano, salt, and pepper, and stir well. Bring the mixture to a boil, stirring occasionally. Reduce the heat to low and simmer gently for 25 to 30 minutes or until the sauce has thickened.

2 Store in an airtight container in the refrigerator for up to two weeks or in the freezer for up to two months.

MAKES 3½ CUPS

¼ cup olive oil

4 garlic cloves, minced

2 shallots, chopped

1 (35-ounce) can crushed tomatoes

3 fresh basil leaves, chopped

1 teaspoon red pepper flakes

½ teaspoon dried oregano

Salt and freshly ground black pepper

Chicken Broth

MAKES 2 QUARTS

2 pounds chicken bones (from about 2 cooked chickens)

1 large onion, unpeeled and quartered

1 large carrot, roughly chopped

2 celery ribs, roughly chopped

1 leek, roughly chopped

2 bay leaves

2 fresh flat-leaf parsley sprigs

2 fresh thyme sprigs

5 whole black peppercorns

Salt and freshly ground black pepper

So why make your own broth? The main reason is that you'll get a richness of flavor in your homemade stock that you just can't buy at the store. Homemade broth has an intense chicken flavor and an unbeatable smell. While the thought of making your own broth may seem intimidating, we promise that it's not! In fact, it requires little attention once all the ingredients hit the pot.

1 Place all of the ingredients except salt and pepper into a 5-quart stockpot and cover with cold water. Set the pot over high heat and bring to a boil. Reduce the heat to low and simmer for 3 to 4 hours. Check the seasoning after a couple of hours and season with salt and pepper to taste.

2 Remove the pot from the heat and let the broth sit for 10 to 15 minutes. Strain the broth through a fine sieve and place in the refrigerator overnight. The next day, skim the coagulated fat off the top of the broth.

 If you don't plan to use your broth within 48 hours, pour the broth into ice cube trays and freeze, then put the broth cubes in zip-top freezer bags. The broth will keep in the freezer for up to three months.

Beef Broth

Store-bought beef broth works just fine, but—just as with chicken broth—it simply doesn't compare in taste to the homemade version. The trick with beef stock is to roast the bones first in order to achieve a nice caramelized flavor.

1 Preheat the oven to 450°F.

2 Put the beef bones, onions, and carrots in the bottom of a 9 x 13-inch casserole dish. Bake, turning occasionally, for about 30 minutes or until the bones are very brown. Let cool for 30 minutes, then drain the fat out of the dish (keep the dish on hand).

3 Put the browned bones, onions, and carrots in a large stockpot. Pour about ½ cup water into the casserole dish, then scrape browned bits off bottom of the dish. Pour this liquid into the soup pot—this liquid holds a ton of flavor! Add the celery, tomato, tomato paste, garlic, parsley, thyme, bay leaf, and peppercorns. Add 12 cups of water and bring the mixture to a boil. Reduce the heat to low, cover, and simmer for 5 hours. Strain the broth, discarding the meat, vegetables, and seasonings.

4 Let the broth cool completely. Transfer to an airtight container and refrigerate overnight. The next day, skim off all the fat that's risen to the surface.

If you don't plan to use your beef broth within 48 hours, pour the broth into ice cube trays and freeze, then put the broth cubes in zip-top freezer bags. The broth will keep in the freezer for up to three months.

MAKES 2 QUARTS

6 pounds beef soup bones (ask butcher for them)

2 medium onions, roughly chopped

3 medium carrots, roughly chopped

3 celery ribs, roughly chopped

1 large tomato, quartered

2 tablespoons tomato paste, thinned with 2 tablespoons water

1 garlic clove, crushed

3 to 4 parsley stems, roughly chopped

½ teaspoon chopped fresh thyme leaves

1 bay leaf

8 whole black peppercorns

Cream of Chicken Soup

MAKES ABOUT 3 CUPS

2 tablespoons vegetable oil

1 medium onion, chopped

2½ tablespoons all-purpose flour

1½ cups whole milk

½ cup heavy cream

1 cup finely shredded roasted chicken (see page 204)

½ tablespoon sugar

½ teaspoon dried thyme

½ teaspoon garlic powder

½ teaspoon salt

½ teaspoon freshly ground black pepper

Creamed soups are often used as a base ingredient in casseroles, and cream of chicken is among the most popular of choices. Trust us when we say that making this soup from scratch and using it in recipes will really make a huge flavor difference by highlighting the freshest ingredients and doing away with preservatives and artificial colorings. This soup is fantastic as a ingredient in recipes, but don't be afraid to make it as a stand-alone dish as well.

✳ ✳ ✳ ✳ ✳

1 Heat the oil in a 3-quart saucepan set over medium-high heat. Add the onion and cook until translucent and soft, about 8 minutes. Gradually stir in the flour, then slowly add the milk and cream, stirring to break up any clumps of flour. Cook, stirring, until the mixture thickens, about 5 minutes. Add the chicken, sugar, thyme, garlic powder, salt, and pepper. Mix well and simmer for 10 minutes.

2 This soup can be stored in the refrigerator for up to two days. Cream-based soups do not freeze well, as they tend to separate when being reheated.

Cream of Mushroom *Soup*

There are some exceptions where homemade just makes good common flavor sense. This recipe boasts a lovely, woody mushroom flavor that doesn't compare to the canned variety. It's perfect for adding to your favorite recipes, such as our Oh Boy! Broccoli Casserole, page 131.

✳   ✳   ✳   ✳   ✳

1   In a large pot set over high heat, bring the broth to a boil.

2   Meanwhile, in a large saucepan set over medium-high heat, melt the butter. Add the leek and mushrooms, and cook, without adding color, for 6 minutes. Sprinkle in the flour and thyme, and cook for 3 to 4 minutes. Let the mixture cool slightly.

3   Gradually whisk the hot stock into the leek and mushroom mixture, making sure to break up any lumps. Add the bay leaf and season with salt and pepper. Return the mixture to a boil. Reduce the heat to low, and simmer gently for 30 to 35 minutes, stirring occasionally.

4   Put the soup in batches into a blender and puree. Pass the blended soup through a fine strainer into a large saucepan. Put the soup over medium-high heat, add the cream, and return to a boil. Season to taste with more salt and pepper.

5   This soup can be stored in the refrigerator for up to two days. Cream-based soups do not freeze well, as they tend to separate when being reheated.

MAKES 3 CUPS

1 quart chicken broth (see page 200)

¼ cup (½ stick) unsalted butter

½ cup roughly chopped leek, white parts only

1 cup roughly chopped white button mushrooms

½ cup all-purpose flour

¾ teaspoon dried thyme

1 bay leaf

½ teaspoon salt, or more as needed

½ teaspoon freshly ground black pepper, or more as needed

½ cup heavy cream

CQ
Roasted Chicken

MAKES 4 SERVINGS

1 (3-pound) whole chicken, giblets removed

1 tablespoon onion powder

Salt and freshly ground black pepper

½ cup (1 stick) unsalted butter, softened

1 celery rib

If you are looking to save money, taking the time to roast your own chicken really can go a long way. Plus this foolproof method makes for a delicious chicken every time. After trying this traditional, scrumptious recipe, don't forget to make your own chicken broth from the chicken bones, which are rich in flavor. Talk about more cluck for your buck.

✳ ✳ ✳ ✳ ✳

1 Preheat the oven to 350°F.

2 Place the chicken in a roasting pan and season it generously, inside and out, with the onion powder, salt, and pepper. Put 3 tablespoons of the butter in the cavity of the chicken. Rub 3 tablespoons of butter on the chicken's skin. Cut the celery into a few pieces and put them in the chicken cavity. Bake for 1 hour 15 minutes, until a meat thermometer inserted into the thickest part of the chicken breast registers 180°F.

3 Remove the roasting pan from the oven. Melt the remaining 2 tablespoons butter in a small saucepan. Baste the chicken with the melted butter and pan drippings. Cover with aluminum foil and allow to rest about 30 minutes before carving.

Acknowledgments

Collectively:

To Michael Lovitt, Brian De los Santos, and Colleen Hammond. From throwing around ideas in Crystal's living room to watching us on *Throwdown! with Bobby Flay*—we would not exist without your talent, support, and generosity. We can't thank you enough for helping us make our dream a reality.

Alexis McClure, you earned your juice bag. Apple or grape?

To Bobby Flay and the crew at Rock Shrimp Productions, for sharing our small, two-person operation with the rest of the nation.

To Carla Glasser, for opening doors to new opportunities, and to Ashley Phillips and Rica Allannic for inviting us in.

Thanks to the Clarkson Potter team: Lauren Shakely, Doris Cooper, Amy Sly, Mark McCauslin, and Alexis Mentor.

And finally, thank you to all of our family, friends, loyal customers, recipe testers, Facebook fans, Twitter followers, and blog readers. You inspire and encourage us to forge ahead. Without your continued support, we could not succeed.

Sandy:

Michael, you are my rock and I love you.

Mom and Dad, thank you for always believing that I can do anything.

My sisters, Yvonne, Yvette, and Kellye—there are no better examples for a little sis than the three of you.

My perfect nieces and nephews, who make me smile every single day.

Crystal, I love sharing a business, a great friendship, and my birthday with you.

The Lovitt family, thank you for your endless support and excitement.

And thank you to my dear friends for being so awesome! I love you all. Smooch!

Crystal:

To my co-Queen Sandy, our journey is just beginning. I can't wait to see all of the places that we will go! And to her other half, Michael, thank you for all the support that you have not only given to Sandy, but also to our company. The two of you exemplify what a true partnership should represent.

To my family, who I adore: thank you for putting the "fun" in dysfunction. I cannot imagine my life without you. (Well I could, but it would be a very sad place without any laughter—and who would want that?) Here's to building even more memories as Maggie and Kris introduce yet another generation of kiddos to our clan.

To Tim, for picking me up and putting the pieces back together.

And last but never least, to the most wonderful group of supportive friends a gal could ever have—from sheer comic relief to shoulders to cry on, from nights at the kitchen to impromptu dance parties. I love you all more than you will ever know.

Index